AN INSPECTOR CALLS

J.B. PRIESTLEY

A GCSE revision guide
...ised and written by Janet Oliver

The right of Janet Oliver to be identified as Author of this Work has been asserted by her in accordance with the Copyright, Designs and Patents Act 1988

First published 2018

ISBN 978-1-9998402-7-3

© Vega Publishing LTD 2018

ACKNOWLEDGEMENTS:

Quotations from 'An Inspector Calls' taken from An Inspector Calls and Other Plays by J.B. Priestley, 2001, London. 'An Inspector Calls © 1947 by J.B. Priestley. Reproduced by permission of Penguin Books Ltd.

The author and publisher are grateful to the copyright holder for permission to use quoted material.

Vega Publishing LTD, 12 Glebe Avenue, Woodford Green, Essex
IG8 9HB United Kingdom

Design by Benedict Nangle

Contents

Introduction - how to use this book 4

Timeline - plot summary 6

Section 1   **Inspector Goole** - character analysis 8

Section 2   **Arthur Birling** - character analysis 14

Section 3   **Sybil Birling** - character analysis 20

Section 4   **Sheila Birling** - character analysis 26

Section 5   **Eric Birling** - character analysis 32

Section 6   **Gerald Croft** - character analysis 38

Section 7   **Eva Smith/Daisy Renton** - character analysis 44

Section 8   **Dramatic Tension** - exploration of the text 50

Section 9   **Generation** - exploration of a theme 56

Section 10   **Lies & Hypocrisy** - exploration of a theme 62

Section 11   **Social Class** - exploration of a theme 68

Section 12   **Social Responsibility** - exploration of a theme 74

Section 13   **Love & Relationships** - exploration of a theme 80

Quotations - recap & revise 86

Glossary - explanation of terms 90

Introduction
How to use this book

'An Inspector Calls' is one of Priestley's most famous plays. It is packed with drama and tension and has entertained audiences for over fifty years. Its universal appeal is obvious but tackling such a wide-ranging play in a short exam is a real challenge.

This guide is written and laid out to help you with your revision of 'An Inspector Calls' and to ensure that your examination response is focused and clear. It is designed to show you how to address the most important elements that the examiner is looking for:

- **Language analysis**
- **Effective use of quotations**
- **Exploration of themes**
- **Understanding of character**
- **How an audience would react to the play**

The book is divided into sections of characters and themes. There is a box at the top of each section which gives a strong, clear overview of the character or theme.

The section is then dealt with using 5-8 key quotations which are in **bold** font. Literary devices are in ***bold italics***.

The analysis of each quotation relates directly to the theme or character. Some of the points are fairly straightforward and some are much more analytical.

The context is added at the end to show how it can be woven into an answer with a relevant quotation. Context means the social, historical and literary influences of the time that Priestley was writing in and how these are reflected in the play.

---

11 Social Class
Exploration of a theme

The theme of social class is at the heart of the play. The plot of the play revolves around how Eva Smith/Daisy Renton, a working class girl, is exploited and abused by members of the wealthy upper classes.

'good solid furniture'
'living in lodgings'

- The opening ***stage directions*** establish the wealth of the Birling family.
- There is a sense of stability and prosperity in the staging and this is enhanced by the props such as **'champagne glasses'**.
- Later, the Inspector describes how Eva is alone and poor: **'living in lodgings'**.
- The word **'lodgings'** suggests temporary, bleak accommodation which ***contrasts*** with the **'good solid furniture'** and reminds the audience about the difference in the life styles between the upper classes and the lower classes.

'Well, it's my duty to keep labour costs down'

- Arthur Birling is forced into answering the Inspector's question about why he refused Eva's request for a wage increase.
- Birling states that he needs to keep **'labour costs down'**. This phrase uses the language of economics which disguises the reality of the situation; by keeping wages down, the wealthy Mr Birling is condemning his workers to lives of poverty and hardship.

Priestley was a socialist and wanted to see society change so that there was a fairer distribution of profit and that workers were treated more fairly. Through Birling's defensive, arrogant words, we see Priestley criticise the capitalist system which helped prop up the upper classes at the expense of the lower classes.

There is also a yellow box entitled 'Grade 9 Exploration' in each chapter. This shows you how you can look at alternative interpretations of the play, which are crucial for gaining a grade of 7 or above.

➡️

Grade 9 Exploration: Look at the text in a different way

<u>Is 'An Inspector Calls' primarily a political play about class?</u>

Yes: Priestley was a committed socialist and wrote the play at the end of the Second World War, when the Labour Party was coming to power with promises of free health service and a fairer, more equitable society. The play consistently reflects Priestley's beliefs as he tries to show the audience that there are still **'millions and millions and millions of Eva Smiths'** to be considered and to take responsibility for.

No: The genre of the play is ambiguous. Priestley follows the formula for a classic whodunnit, a detective story where the audience has to guess who the criminal is. However, the whodunnit is not the definitive genre and 'An Inspector Calls' could fit into the category of a morality play. These were plays performed in the Middle Ages which taught audiences how to behave through repentance the deadly sins and certainly the Birlings and Gerald between them represent all seven deadly sins. Yet perhaps the play is primarily a portrayal of family relationships; after all, the audience is fully engaged as we watch the relationships between the characters change throughout the story.

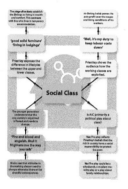

Look out for the colourful mindmap. It condenses four main points from the chapter, including the Grade 9 Exploration box, into four strands. The information is in a shortened format; if you want to keep your revision really focused, use the mind map to make sure you remember the key features of the chapter.

⬅️

The sample essay follows. This is based on a 4 paragraph formula which answers the question clearly and analytically. The font is small as there is so much detail but, if you are wondering what a top level answer looks like, do read it carefully.

➡️

Sample GCSE Exam Question & Answer

Q: Explore how far 'An Inspector Calls' is a political play about social class.

☑ **Start with the point that the division of social class is established from the opening of the play**

The theme of social class is at the heart of the play. The plot of the play revolves around how Eva Smith/Daisy Renton, a working class girl, is exploited and abused by members of the wealthy upper classes. This is shown from the opening **stage directions** which establish the wealth of the Birling family: **'good solid furniture'**. There is a sense of stability and prosperity in the staging and this is enhanced by the props such as **'champagne glasses'**. Later, the Inspector describes how Eva is alone and poor: **'living in lodgings'**. The word **'lodgings'** suggests temporary, bleak accommodation which **contrasts** with the **'good solid furniture'** and reminds the audience about the difference in the life styles between the upper classes and the lower classes.

☑ **Move to the point that Priestley uses the characters to show how the lower classes are exploited and abused**

Mr Birling see it as his duty to exploit the working classes, being forced into answering the Inspector's question about why he refused Eva's request for a wage increase saying **'Well, it's my duty to keep labour costs down'**. As Birling states that he needs to keep **'labour costs down'**, this phrase uses the language of economics which disguises the reality of the situation; by keeping wages down, the wealthy Mr Birling is condemning his workers to lives of poverty and hardship. It is interesting that Birling sees his actions as his **'duty'**; while the Inspector's, and Priestley's, duty is a desire to change society, Birling's duty is simply to make more money. Priestley was a socialist and wanted to see society change so that there was a fairer distribution of profit and that workers were treated more fairly. Through Birling's defensive, arrogant words, we see Priestley criticise the capitalist system which helped prop up the upper classes at the expense of the lower classes. Similarly, Priestley uses Mrs Birling to show how she despises the working classes. Mrs Birling dismisses Eva Smith as **'girls of that class'**. She sees Eva as just one of many working girls. By grouping the girls together, she shows a lack of humanity; she sees them as a type, not as individuals. There is a sense of snobbery in the **determiner 'that'** which distances herself from them. Society in 1912 was strictly controlled with a rigid hierarchy of social class; Mrs Birling firmly believes in this social system and this belief is evident in her choice of language.

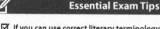
Essential Exam Tips

☑ If you can use correct literary terminology (metaphor/imperative verbs etc), do use it! It makes your response much more convincing.

☑ Start revising for the exams early. Revising in 10 minutes bursts from the end of Year 10 can make a huge difference and reduces the last minute panic before your exams.

⬅️

Below that there is a box with essential exam tips: lots of good ideas and reminders that will help you on exam day.

At the back of the book, there is a glossary of all the literary terms with examples and there's a list of the quotations with the act references. You really don't need to learn these references; they are only included to help you find the place in the play for your own revision.

Timeline
Plot Summary

In 'An Inspector Calls', Priestley uses the three unities of classical Greek theatre: unity of action, unity of time and unity of place. This means that the story unfolds in real time with no gaps so that the audience is completely engrossed in the experience of watching the Inspector expose the Birlings' involvement in Eva Smith's death. There are recounts of events that happened before the dinner party which add to our understanding of the characters and strengthens Priestley's message.

Act 1

- The play opens as the Birling family are having a dinner to celebrate the engagement of Sheila Birling to Gerald Croft.

- Arthur Birling makes self-satisfied speeches about how war will never happen and how business, not a sense of community, is important.

- The sound of a door bell cuts across one of these speeches and Inspector Goole arrives. He tells them that he is there to investigate the suicide of a young girl who has swallowed disinfectant.

- Inspector Goole shows Mr Birling a photograph of the dead girl, Eva Smith. Mr Birling relates the story of how Eva was one of the workers at his factory who organised a strike in an attempt to be given higher wages. The strike was soon over and Mr Birling dismissed Eva Smith.

- The Inspector then shows Sheila the photograph of the dead girl. Upset, Sheila confesses how she had Eva dismissed from her new position as a shop girl.

- Gerald reacts to Eva's change of name to Daisy Renton. It is clear that he too knew the dead girl.

Act 2

- Gerald reveals how he met Daisy in a bar and then kept her as his mistress for some months.

- After this confession, Sheila returns her engagement ring to Gerald.

- The Inspector turns his attention to Sybil Birling. It is her turn to reveal that she knew Daisy. Daisy had come to the charitable organisation of which Mrs Birling is a prominent member. Daisy was pregnant and desperate but Mrs Birling used her influence to turn her away without help.

- Mrs Birling announces that helping Daisy was not her responsibility; it was the responsibility of the unknown father.

- As she says this, Eric Birling walks in.

Act 3

- Eric tells the Inspector and his family how he got Daisy pregnant and then stole money from his father's firm to support her.

- The Inspector tells the assembled family that they all had a part to blame in Eva/Daisy's death. He also tells them that society has a responsibility to look after everyone. The Inspector then leaves.

- Gerald returns and raises suspicions as to whether Inspector Goole is a genuine police officer.

- Mr Birling makes a phone call that confirms that the Inspector is a 'fake'. A second telephone call confirms that no girl died in the infirmary that night from swallowing disinfectant.

- Arthur, Sybil and Gerald are all relieved and dismiss their earlier guilt. Sheila and Eric continue to feel remorse.

- At the end, the telephone rings; a young girl has just committed suicide by drinking disinfectant and an inspector is on his way to investigate.

1 Inspector Goole
Character analysis

Inspector Goole is the mysterious character who turns the lives of the self-satisfied Birlings upside down by exposing their involvement in the death of Eva Smith. The Inspector raises ideas of private and public responsibility and also acts as an effective dramatic device.

'sharp ring of a front door bell'

- A ***stage direction*** of a ringing door bell introduces the Inspector.

- The bell cuts across Mr Birling's speech which outlines his views on **'community and all that nonsense'**. The **'sharp'** ring *foreshadows* the impact that the Inspector will have on Mr Birling's life as it demonstrates how the Inspector has the power to interrupt Mr Birling and to challenge him.

- The ***stage direction*** stops Mr Birling and the sound also jolts the audience. It signals a turning point in the play.

'He says his name is Inspector Goole'

- The Inspector claims that his name is **'Goole'**.

- The unusual name reflects the odd nature of this police officer and raises questions about the function of the Inspector. **'Goole'** is a play on the word 'ghoul', suggesting that he is a supernatural being, perhaps sent by the dead Eva to force the Birlings to take responsibility for her death.

'one line of enquiry at a time'

- The Inspector takes charge of the enquiry.

- Inspector Goole controls the ***pace*** of the story by interviewing one person at a time. He is a dramatic device used by Priestley to expose the crimes of Birlings and the Crofts in a methodical, ruthlessly efficient manner.

'Burnt her inside out, of course'

- Investigating an incident, Inspector Goole establishes the victim and the nature of her death: that Eva swallowed disinfectant which **'burnt her inside out, of course'**.

- The graphic **vocabulary** of the corrosive liquid destroying Eva's body is shocking to the Birlings and also to the audience. The matter-of-fact **interjection 'of course'** only highlights just how appalling the death was; there was no doubt at all about the fatal outcome of her actions.

By establishing the crime, Priestley follows the formula for a classic whodunnit, a detective story where the audience has to guess who the criminal is. However, the whodunnit is not the definitive genre; 'An Inspector Calls' could fit into the category of a morality play, a political play or a drama about family life.

'Don't stammer and yammer at me again, man. I'm losing all patience with you people'

- The Inspector becomes impatient with Mr Birling's interruptions and tells him to be quiet.

- He shows a complete lack of respect for his social superior, Mr Birling, through his use of the **imperatives**. This lack of deference (respect) is also seen in the dismissive address of **'man'**.

- The **colloquial phrase 'stammer and yammer'** reflects the Inspector's deep anger and disgust at the Birlings. This use of North-Eastern **dialect** helps create a sense of a real person.

Society in 1912 was organised by an inflexible hierarchy based on power and class. Mr Birling, as a member of the middle class, is socially superior to the Inspector but the way the Inspector talks to Mr Birling shows how the Inspector, and Priestley, challenges this social system.

- The Inspector's final speech warns that, if society does not learn lessons of public and private responsibility for the poor and the weak, then it will be taught these lessons in **'fire and blood and anguish'**.

- The *syndetic list* of violent destructive *nouns* signals a clear warning to the Birlings and to the audience that horror lies ahead of them unless they change their ways.

- The **'fire and blood and anguish'** could refer to battlefields of WW1. Alternatively, the Inspector could be referring to the fires and pain of hell where the Birlings will be punished in an after-life for their sins in this world.

> The Inspector here acts as Priestley's mouthpiece. As a socialist, Priestley firmly believed that society should be organised in a fair and equitable way. The Inspector's warning is very relevant to the 1945/6 audience that, without a fairer society, the horrors of World War 1 and World War 2 will be repeated.

 Grade 9 Exploration: Look at the character in a different way

Is the Inspector immensely powerful in changing the Birlings?

Yes: Priestley's *stage directions* reveal an incredibly influential character; for example, the Inspector should have an **'impression of massiveness'**. Other *stage directions* show his control as he **'takes charge' 'cutting in'** and forces all the Birlings, including the impregnable Mrs Birling, to admit their part in Eva's death. Even the lighting reflects his power as when he enters, it becomes **'brighter and harder'**, destroying the cosy, intimate atmosphere. In Stephen Daldry's famous production, the Birlings' house is on stilts and collapses at the end of the play after the Inspector's investigation. It is a very clear and dramatic demonstration to the audience of just how much of an impact the Inspector has.

No: The Inspector does not force the Birlings to confess and, in Sheila and Eric's cases, change. He simply acts as a guide, and merely shows the characters their faults and their role in the treatment of Eva. Indeed, when Sheila runs out of the room, crying, the Inspector states: **'I haven't done anything. She is upsetting herself'**. Priestley uses elements of Greek theatre in his play and the Inspector acts as the *chorus*, commenting on the action and the characters. He is not necessarily instrumental himself in affecting change.

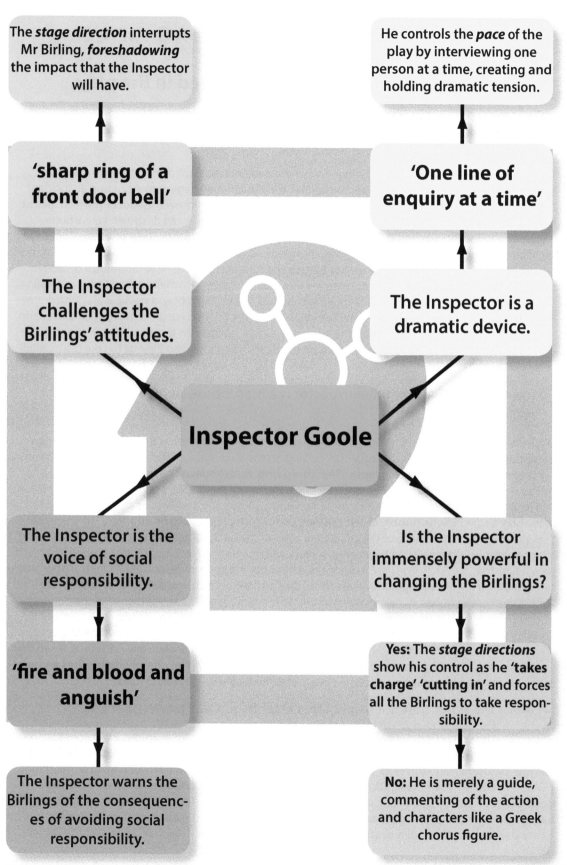

The *stage direction* interrupts Mr Birling, *foreshadowing* the impact that the Inspector will have.

'sharp ring of a front door bell'

The Inspector challenges the Birlings' attitudes.

He controls the *pace* of the play by interviewing one person at a time, creating and holding dramatic tension.

'One line of enquiry at a time'

The Inspector is a dramatic device.

Inspector Goole

The Inspector is the voice of social responsibility.

'fire and blood and anguish'

The Inspector warns the Birlings of the consequences of avoiding social responsibility.

Is the Inspector immensely powerful in changing the Birlings?

Yes: The *stage directions* show his control as he 'takes charge' 'cutting in' and forces all the Birlings to take responsibility.

No: He is merely a guide, commenting of the action and characters like a Greek chorus figure.

Sample GCSE Exam Question & Answer

Q: Explore how the Inspector is presented in the play.

☑ Make the point that the Inspector is presented as a man in charge of an investigation

The Inspector is announced to the Birlings and to the audience as a policeman; the servant Edna states that **'he says his name is Inspector Goole'**. He immediately begins investigating an incident by establishing the victim and the nature of her death: that Eva swallowed disinfectant which **'burnt her inside out, of course'**. The graphic *vocabulary* of the corrosive liquid destroying Eva's body is shocking to the Birlings and also the audience. The matter-of-fact *interjection* **'of course'** only highlights just how appalling the death was; there was no doubt at all about the fatal outcome of her actions. By establishing the crime, Priestley follows the formula for a classic whodunnit, a detective story where the audience has to guess who the criminal is. However, the whodunnit is not the definitive genre; 'An Inspector Calls' could fit into the category of a morality play, a political play or a drama about family life. Indeed, the unusual name of 'Goole' reflects the odd nature of this police officer and raises questions about the function of the Inspector. 'Goole' is a play on the word 'ghoul', suggesting that he is a supernatural being, perhaps sent by the dead Eva to force the Birlings to take responsibility for her death.

☑ Develop the point that the Inspector is a man whose purpose is to teach responsibility

The Inspector's impact is clear even before he steps on stage. A *stage direction* of the **'sharp ring of a front door bell'** introduces the Inspector, cutting across Mr Birling's speech which outlines his views on **'community and all that nonsense'**. The **'sharp ring'** *foreshadows* the impact that the Inspector will have on Mr Birling's life as it demonstrates how the Inspector has the power to interrupt Mr Birling and to challenge him. The sound stops Mr Birling and also jolts the audience; it signals a turning point in the play as the Birlings' bubble of self-satisfied complacency begins to be attacked. The Inspector then proceeds to expose each of the characters' roles in the death of Eva Smith/Daisy Renton, forcing the characters to acknowledge their sense of responsibility until he reaches his final speech in which he predicts that, if society does not learn lessons of public and private responsibility for the poor and the weak, then it will be taught these lessons in **'fire and blood and anguish'**. The *syndetic list* of violent destructive *nouns* signals a clear warning to the Birlings and to the audience of the dangers in ignoring this social responsibility. The Inspector here acts as Priestley's mouthpiece. As a socialist, Priestley firmly believed that society should be organised in a fair and equitable way. The Inspector's warning is very relevant to the 1945/6 audience that, without a fairer society, the horrors of World War 1 and World War 2 will be repeated. Alternatively, the Inspector could be referring to the fires and pain of hell where the Birlings will be punished in an after-life for their sins in this world.

☑ Make the point that the Inspector is established as a powerful man

Priestley's *stage directions* reveal an incredibly influential character; for example, the Inspector should have an **'impression of massiveness'**. Other *stage directions* show his control as he **'takes charge' 'cutting in'** and forces all the Birlings, including the impregnable Mrs Birling, to admit their part in Eva's death. Even the lighting reflects his power as, when he enters, it becomes **'brighter and harder'**, destroying the cosy, intimate atmosphere. In Stephen Daldry's famous production, the Birlings' house is on stilts and collapses at the end of the play after the Inspector's investigation. It is a very clear and dramatic demonstration to the audience of just how much of an impact the Inspector has. However, this is only one view and it could be argued that the Inspector does not force the Birlings to confess and, in Sheila and Eric's cases, change. He simply acts as a guide, and merely shows the characters their faults and their role in the treatment of Eva. Indeed, when Sheila runs out of the room, crying, the Inspector states: **'I haven't done anything. She is upsetting herself'**. Priestley uses elements of Greek theatre in his play and the Inspector acts as the ***chorus***, commenting on the action and the characters. He is not necessarily instrumental himself in affecting change.

☑ Move to another point; examine how far the Inspector is a dramatic device

Priestley does, in part, use the character of Inspector Goole as a dramatic device. He controls the ***pace*** of the story by interviewing one person at a time - **'one line of enquiry at a time'**- and so exposing the crimes of Birlings and the Crofts in a methodical, ruthlessly efficient manner. Yet we do get a definite sense of a real character, not just a dramatic device. The Inspector becomes impatient with Mr Birling's interruptions and tells him to be quiet: **'Don't stammer and yammer at me, man. I'm losing all patience with you people.'** The ***colloquial phrase*** **'stammer and yammer'** reflects the Inspector's deep anger and disgust at the Birlings while the use of North-Eastern ***dialect*** helps create a sense of a real person. He shows a complete lack of respect for his social superior, Mr Birling, through his use of the ***imperatives*** and this lack of deference (respect) is also seen in the dismissive address of **'man'**. Society in 1912 was organised by an inflexible hierarchy based on power and class. Mr Birling, as a member of the middle class, is socially superior to the Inspector but the way the Inspector talks to Mr Birling shows how the Inspector, and Priestley, challenge this social system. At the end of the play, there can be little doubt that this Inspector is a character that is complex and one that has a powerful impact on the Birlings and Gerald and, almost certainly, the audience as well.

Essential Exam Tips

☑ Read the play on your own at home. Listen to audio books of the play as well.

☑ Refer to different places within the play. For example, don't just write about the start of the play as that doesn't show the examiner that you have a good understanding of the whole play.

Arthur Birling is a wealthy manufacturer who takes great pride in his business success. He is head of the household and, at the start of the play, is a complacent man in a position of control.

'I'm talking as a hard-headed, practical man of business'

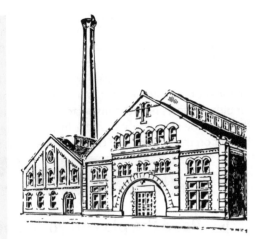

- Arthur Birling declares himself to be a sensible, pragmatic businessman. He *repeats* this phrase in Act 1, showing that he takes great pride in his position as a factory owner.

- The *tone* of pride in the *adjectives* **'hard-headed'** and **'practical'** reveals that he sees these qualities as admirable ones, and the phrase **'man of business'** shows that Priestley is establishing Arthur Birling as a *symbol* of capitalism.

Capitalism was the economic system which shaped society in 1912. Capitalism meant that rich landowners and factory owners were able to control the labour force, resulting in profit for those in control but often poor living and working conditions for the workers.

'unsinkable, absolutely unsinkable'

- Mr Birling declares the Titanic to be unsinkable.
- He *repeats* this opinion, which he presents as a fact, with the *intensifier* 'absolutely' showing his complete confidence in his judgement.

The Titanic famously sank in 1912, the year that the play is set in. The watching audience of 1945/46 knew this and so Priestley uses *dramatic irony* to show how flawed Arthur Birling's judgement is. From this point onwards, we do not trust anything that he says.

'community and all that nonsense'

- Mr Birling states that we only have a responsibility to ourselves and to our families; he dismisses the idea of community and social responsibility as **'non-sense'**.

- There is an arrogance and an ignorance in his dismissive, contemptuous *tone*.

> **Priestley was a socialist and believed that a fairer way of organising society and industry would result in a better world. We already distrust Mr Birling's judgement because of his comments on the Titanic, and here Priestley shows how misguided Mr Birling is.**

'Well, it's my duty to keep labour costs down'

- Arthur Birling is forced into answering the Inspector's question about why he refused Eva's request for a wage increase.

- The *interjection* 'well' suggests that Mr Birling is reluctant to justify himself, yet he does give reasons for his actions, showing that the Inspector has power over him.

- Birling states that he needs to keep **'labour costs down'**. He uses the language of economics which hides the reality of the situation; by keeping wages down, Birling is condemning his workers to lives of poverty and hardship.

- Birling sees his actions as his **'duty'**; while the Inspector's, and Priestley's, duty is to change society, Birling's duty is to make more money.

'I've got to cover this up as soon as I can. You damned fool-'

- Mr Birling's first instinct when he hears about Eric's activities of stealing money is to **'cover this up'**. Priestley shows us how Arthur Birling's hypocrisy is deep-rooted. It does not seem to matter to him that his son is in such a desperate position that he is stealing to pay for his unborn child; he is more concerned with his company's position. Mr Birling's earlier proud declaration that he is **'hard-headed'** and **'practical'** is exposed here for what it is: a lack of compassion and empathy.

- He snaps at Eric that he is a **'damned fool'**; this insult is patronising and vicious, and shows how Mr Birling despises his son. He makes little effort to understand Eric's actions, and instead verbally attacks him, showing himself to be an inadequate father.

- At the end, when it is realised that the Inspector was a 'fake', Birling sneers at his children for still being troubled by the evening's events.

- He is a character who has learned nothing from the events; he dismisses a girl's suicide and his part in it as **'a lot of stuff'**. This callous off-hand phrase shows that he is cold and uncaring.

- Birling shows his pretensions to achieve a higher social standing in his desire to avoid a **'public scandal'** that could damage his chances at moving up the social ladder by being given a knighthood. At the end of the play, he is un-changed - as snobbish, arrogant and unlikeable as at the start.

Pre-world war society in 1912 was strictly controlled with a rigid hierarchy of social class. Despite being rich, Mr Birling does not have the social status he craves and is desperate to achieve this knighthood; Priestley condemns this social climbing.

 ## Grade 9 Exploration: Look at the character in a different way

Is Arthur Birling a completely unchanged character?

Yes: Any wish to change the situation stems from his fear that he is about to be pub-licly exposed, not because he feels any shame or remorse. The fact that he defines any regret in monetary terms - **'thousands'** of pounds - shows that he is still seeing the world purely in terms of financial gain and loss.

No: In Act 3, Arthur Birling says **(unhappily) 'I'd give thousands- yes thousands'** to change the course of events, showing some regret here for the consequences of his actions. The *stage direction* **'unhappily'** and the *fragmented speech* indicated through the *dashes* suggests a change from the character at the start who is very pleased with himself and his life; he is now disturbed, with his confidence shaken by the events. The *repetition* of **'thousands'** shows the extent to which he feels re-morse and wishes that he could change the past.

Priestley drew upon conventions of morality plays. These were plays per-formed in the Middle Ages which taught audiences how to behave through the repentance of the deadly sins. Arthur Birling represents the deadly sins of avarice (love of money) and pride, but he does not repent and is essentially unchanged at the end of the play.

He *repeats* this phrase, showing he is proud of his position as a sensible businessman.

Mr Birling's certainty about the Titanic being unsinkable shows that his views are suspect and the audience does not trust him or his opinions.

'I'm talking as a hard-headed, practical man of business'

'Unsinkable - absolutely unsinkable'

Mr Birling is a *symbol* of capitalism.

Priestley undercuts Mr Birling's views.

Arthur Birling

Mr Birling refuses to accept responsibility.

Is Arthur Birling a completely unchanged character?

'They just won't try to... see the difference between a lot of stuff like this coming out in private and a downright public scandal'

Yes: Any wish to change the situation stems from his fear that he is about to be publicly exposed, not because he feels any shame or remorse.

He is more concerned with his reputation and social position than a dead girl or his unhappy son.

No: Mr Birling says **(unhappily)** **'I'd give thousands- yes thousands'** to change the course of events, showing regret here for the consequences of his actions.

Sample GCSE Exam Question & Answer

Q: Explore how Arthur Birling and his views are presented in the play.

☑ Make the point that Arthur is a *symbol* of capitalism

Arthur Birling declares himself from the outset to be a sensible, pragmatic businessman, stating that **'I'm talking as a hard-headed, practical man of business'** and he *repeats* this phrase in Act 1, showing that he takes great satisfaction in his position as a factory owner. The *tone* of pride in the *adjectives* **'hard-headed'** and **'practical'** reveals that he sees these qualities as admirable ones, and the phrase **'man of business'** shows that Priestley is establishing Arthur Birling as a *symbol* of capitalism. Capitalism was the economic system which shaped society in 1912. Capitalism meant that rich landowners and factory owners were able to control the labour force, resulting in profit for those in control but often poor living and working conditions for the workers. However, Priestley ensures that the audience does not respect Mr Birling as he pronounces the Titanic to be **'unsinkable, absolutely unsinkable'**. He *repeats* this opinion, which he presents as a fact, with the *intensifier* **'absolutely'** showing his complete confidence in his judgement. The Titanic famously sank in 1912, the year that the play is set in. The watching audience of 1945/46 knew this and so Priestley uses *dramatic irony* to show how flawed Arthur Birling's judgement is. From this point onwards, we do not trust anything that he says.

☑ Move to the point that Arthur is presented as a man who lacks social responsibility

Arthur Birling certainly has strong opinions as he states that we only have a responsibility to ourselves and to our families; he dismisses the idea of social responsibility as **'community and all that non-sense'**. There is an arrogance and an ignorance in his dismissive, contemptuous *tone*. Priestley was a socialist and believed that a fairer way of organising society and industry would result in a better world. We already distrust Mr Birling's judgement because of his comments on the Titanic being **'unsinkable'**, and here Priestley shows how misguided Mr Birling is. Later, Arthur Birling is forced into answering the Inspector's question about why he refused Eva's request for a wage increase, saying **'Well, it's my duty to keep labour costs down'**. The *interjection* **'well'** suggests that Mr Birling is reluctant to justify himself, yet he does give reasons for his actions, showing that the Inspector has power over him. Birling states that he needs to keep **'labour costs down'**. This phrase uses the language of economics which disguises the reality of the situation; by keeping wages down, Birling is condemning his workers to lives of poverty and hardship. It is interesting that Birling sees his actions as his **'duty'**; while the Inspector's, and Priestley's, duty is a desire to change society, Birling's duty is simply to make more money. Through Birling's defensive, arrogant words, we see Priestley criticise the capitalist system that he saw as destructive and unfair.

☑ Make the point that Mr Birling is presented as a poor parent and a hypocrite

Mr Birling does not redeem himself with the audience by presenting himself as a caring father. Mr Birling's first instinct when he hears about Eric's activities of stealing money is to conceal it: **'I've got to cover this up as soon as I can. You damned fool-'**. He is far more interested in his social standing and his company's reputation than in the emotional trauma of his son. Priestley shows us how Arthur Birling's hypocrisy is deep-rooted. It does not seem to matter to Arthur that his son is in such desperate position that he is stealing to pay for his unborn child; he is more concerned with his company's position. Mr Birling's earlier proud declaration that he is **'hard-headed'** and **'practical'** is exposed here for what it is: a lack of compassion and empathy. He snaps at Eric that he is a **'damned fool'**; this insult is patronising and vicious, and shows how Mr Birling despises his son. He makes little effort to understand Eric's actions and instead verbally attacks him, showing himself to be an inadequate father.

☑ Explore whether Arthur Birling changes at all during the course of the play

It seems that Arthur does change as a character throughout the play. In Act 3, Arthur Birling says **(unhappily) 'I'd give thousands- yes thousands'** to change the course of events, showing some regret here for the consequences of his actions. The ***stage direction* 'unhappily'** and the ***fragmented speech*** indicated through the **dash** suggests a change from the character at the start who is very pleased with himself and his life; he is now disturbed, with his confidence shaken by the events. The ***repetition*** of **'thousands'** shows the extent to which he feels remorse and wishes that he could change the past. Yet it could be argued that any wish to change the situation stems from his fear that he is about to be publicly exposed, not because he feels any shame or remorse. The fact that he defines any regret in monetary terms - **'thousands'** of pounds - shows that he is still seeing the world purely in terms of financial gain and loss. Priestley drew upon conventions of morality plays. These were plays performed in the Middle Ages which taught audiences how to behave through repentance of the deadly sins. Arthur Birling represents the deadly sins of avarice (love of money) and pride, but he does not repent and is essentially unchanged at the end of the play.

 # Essential Exam Tips

- ☑ Watch a couple of films or TV dramas set in the Edwardian period such as 'Titanic' or 'Downton Abbey'. These will give you a feel for the time period that the play is set in.

- ☑ Try to weave points about context into your answer when you are writing about a character or theme. Don't just bolt the context on at the end or add it in a completely separate paragraph.

3 Sybil Birling
Character analysis

Sybil Birling is a cold, snobbish woman who is presented unsympathetically throughout the play. Her refusal to help Eva Smith/Daisy Renton is the final event which leads to Eva killing herself.

'As if a girl of that sort would ever refuse money!'

- Mrs Birling laughs at the idea of Eva/Daisy turning down the stolen money from Eric, yet this is exactly what Eva did.

- She sees Eva as just one of many working girls, not as an individual. There is a sense of snobbery in the **determiner** *'that'* which distances herself from Eva. Yet Eva is shown as a girl of strong morals, refusing to accept the money which came from crime. Eva is seen as morally superior to Mrs Birling with an integrity (honesty) that the older woman lacks.

Society in 1912 was strictly controlled with a rigid hierarchy of social class. Mrs Birling firmly believes in this social system and this belief is evident in her choice of language. Priestley challenges the rigid class system which assumed that those born into a high class were 'better' than the working class.

(with dignity)'We've done a great deal of useful work in helping deserving cases''she seemed to be...not a good case'

- Mrs Birling is complacent and self-satisfied in her role as head of a charitable organisation, helping the poor but turning Eva/Daisy away.

- The **stage direction** **'with dignity'** shows her sense of self-importance. Her idea of compassion for others is completely linked to her status as a lady of a high social class.

- She makes a point that she has helped **'deserving cases'**. This tells us that she and the other upper class ladies on the committee make moral judgements about those who come to them for help, deciding who deserves charity. It is this self-satisfied hypocrisy that Priestley challenges through the portrayal of Mrs Birling and her cold-hearted attitude to the vulnerable Eva/Daisy.

By the time Eva went to the charity committee for help, she would have been desperate as in 1912 there was very little state help for those in trouble. Unmarried mothers were despised as women of loose morals at this time; Mrs Birling's attitude reflects contemporary attitudes.

- Mrs Birling states that the man responsible for Eva/Daisy's pregnancy should be forced to publicly admit his guilt.

- Mrs Birling's language is cold and pompous; the **verb 'compelled'** suggests a sense of bullying and this is reinforced by the sense of a witch hunt in the public humiliation that she wants for this unknown young man.

- Her view on responsibility is that of public shaming. However, when it is her son who is exposed, she immediately backtracks, showing her deep-set hypocrisy.

- This is a dramatic moment for the audience as it ends Act 2 with a sense of **climax**. We are expecting Eric's imminent arrival as we, like Sheila, can see that it is Eric who will be exposed as the mysterious father.

(agitated) 'I don't believe it. I **won't** believe it'

- At the end of Act 2, Sybil Birling refuses to believe that her son is involved with Eva/Daisy and the pregnancy.

- The **auxiliary verbs 'don't'** and then, more emphatically **'won't'**, shows her denial of the situation. Mrs Birling only believes what it suits her to believe, what is comfortable for her. The Inspector is forcing her to see the unpleasant reality of her son's behaviour and she resists this.

- The **stage direction 'agitated'** shows that her complacency has been rocked.

Priestley used the conventions of Greek theatre, using Aristotle's Three Unities: unities of place, time and action. This means that the play happens in real time in one, unchanging place and ensures that the audience can clearly see the **contrast** between her assured confidence at the start of the play and her shaken emotions in Act 3.

'Besides, you're not the type- you don't get drunk'

- In Act 3, Sybil Birling is still in denial about her son's behaviour.

- Her words reveal her ignorance and her continued tendency to categorise people as she says **'you're not the type'**. She has not changed at all since the start of the play.

- Her *fragmented speech* shows her anxiety as she is forced to confront the truth that the audience has seen since Act 1: that her son drinks too much. She is seen as an inadequate mother here, blind to Eric's drinking problems.

'Well, why shouldn't we?'

- At the end of the play, Sheila is worried that her parents are behaving as if nothing has happened and her mother asks **'Well, why shouldn't we?'**

- Mrs Birling has learned nothing from the Inspector and her complacent question shows her arrogant presumption that she can return to her old life without any further responsibility.

 ## Grade 9 Exploration: Look at the character in a different way

Is Mrs Birling a terrible person?

Yes: Her own position in society is incredibly privileged and she abuses this by turning down Eva's desperate last plea for help. She knew Eva had nowhere else to turn but still refused her help, based on her prejudices and her snobbish pride. The inspector tells us several times that Eva died a violent death that **'burnt her inside out'** to remind us of the consequences of Sybil Birling's snobbery. She is a detestable character.

No: The audience is given a sense of a real closeness and affection between Sybil and Sheila at the start as they are united in their excitement of the engagement. We should also remember that Mrs Birling is a product of her time; brought up in the Victorian era, she would have been instilled with a sense of innate snobbery, and her parenting of Eric and Sheila would have been defined by this upbringing. She also, tellingly, says to Sheila that Sheila will have to allow Gerald to work long hours away from her: **'you'll have to get used to that, just as I had'**. In 1912 British society, women's lives were restricted to the domestic sphere; no wonder she is narrow-minded, snobbish and petty.

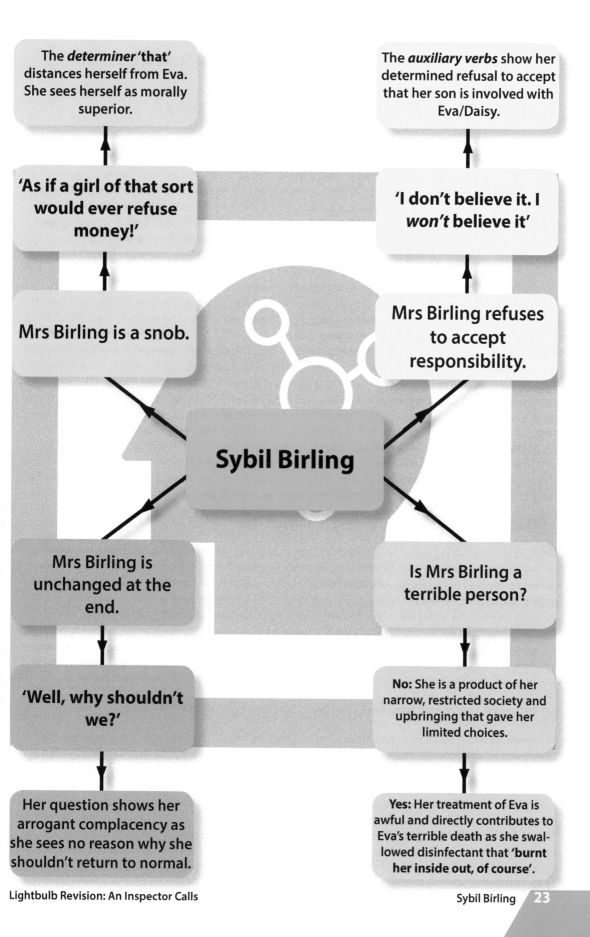

The *determiner* 'that' distances herself from Eva. She sees herself as morally superior.

The *auxiliary verbs* show her determined refusal to accept that her son is involved with Eva/Daisy.

'As if a girl of that sort would ever refuse money!'

'I don't believe it. I *won't* believe it'

Mrs Birling is a snob.

Mrs Birling refuses to accept responsibility.

Sybil Birling

Mrs Birling is unchanged at the end.

Is Mrs Birling a terrible person?

'Well, why shouldn't we?'

No: She is a product of her narrow, restricted society and upbringing that gave her limited choices.

Her question shows her arrogant complacency as she sees no reason why she shouldn't return to normal.

Yes: Her treatment of Eva is awful and directly contributes to Eva's terrible death as she swallowed disinfectant that '**burnt her inside out, of course**'.

Sample GCSE Exam Question & Answer

Q: How is Sybil Birling presented in the play?

☑ Make the point that Mrs Birling is presented as a privileged lady

Mrs Birling is presented as a woman born into a privileged position and as such is very conscious about her status. Society in 1912 was strictly controlled with a rigid hierarchy of social class and the snobbish Mrs Birling firmly believes in this social system. This belief is evident in her choice of language as she laughs at the idea of Eva/Daisy turning down the stolen money from Eric, saying **'as if a girl of that sort would ever refuse money!'** She sees Eva as just one of many working girls, not as an individual. There is a sense of snobbery in the *determiner* **'that'** which distances herself from Eva. Yet Eva is shown as a girl of strong morals, refusing to accept the money which came from crime. She is morally superior to Mrs Birling, with an integrity (honesty) that the older woman lacks, and, through the portrayal of the honest Eva and the unpleasant Mrs Birling, Priestley challenges the rigid class system which assumed that those born into a high class were 'better' than the working class. Mrs Birling is also seen as complacent and self-satisfied in her role as head of a charitable organisation: (**with dignity)'We've done a great deal of useful work in helping deserving cases'**. The *stage direction* **'with dignity'** shows her sense of self-importance. Her idea of compassion for others is completely linked to her status as a lady of high social class and she makes a point that she has helped **'deserving cases'** but that **'she (Eva) seemed to be...not a good case'**. This tells us that she and the other upper class ladies on the committee make moral judgements about those who come to them for help, deciding who deserves charity. It is this self-satisfied hypocrisy that Priestley challenges through the portrayal of the cold-hearted Mrs Birling as, by the time Eva went to the charity committee for help, she would have been desperate. There was very little state help for those in trouble in 1912 and unmarried mothers were despised as women of loose morals at this time. Mrs Birling's attitude reflects these contemporary views which Priestley condemns as callous, arrogant and socially irresponsible.

☑ Make the point that Mrs Birling is a hypocrite

Mrs Birling continues to show her unpleasant side as she goes on to state that the man responsible for Eva/Daisy's pregnancy should be forced to publicly admit his guilt and that he should be **'compelled to confess in public his responsibility'**. Her language is cold and pompous; the *verb* **'compelled'** suggests a sense of bullying and this is reinforced by the sense of a witch hunt in the public humiliation that she wants for this unknown young man. Her view on responsibility is that of public shaming. However, when it is her son who is exposed, she immediately backtracks, showing her deep-set hypocrisy. As Mrs Birling ploughs on with her self-satisifed, superior opinions, this is a dramatic moment for the audience as it ends Act 2 with a sense of *climax*. We are expecting Eric's imminent arrival as we, like Sheila, can see that it is Eric who will be exposed as the mysterious father.

☑ Move to the point that Mrs Birling is shaken by the revelations

At the end of Act 2, Sybil Birling refuses to believe that her son is involved with Eva/Daisy and the pregnancy as she states **(agitated) I don't believe it. I *won't* believe it'**. The *auxiliary verbs* **'don't'** and then, more emphatically, **'won't'**, show her denial of the situation. Mrs Birling only believes what it suits her to believe, what is comfortable for her. The Inspector is forcing her to see the unpleasant reality of her son's behaviour and she resists this but the *stage direction* **'agitated'** shows that her complacency has been rocked. Priestley followed the conventions of Greek theatre, using Aristotle's Three Unities: unities of place, time and action. This means that the play happens in real time in one, unchanging place. The effect of this is that the audience can clearly see the *contrast* between her assured confidence at the start of the play and her shaken emotions in Act 3. This lack of composure is also seen when she tries to deny Eric's drinking, saying **'besides, you're not the type- you don't get drunk-'**. Her words reveal her ignorance and her continued tendency to categorise people- **"you're not the type'**. She has not changed at all since the start of the play yet her *fragmented speech* shows her anxiety as she is forced to confront the truth that the audience has seen since Act 1: that her son drinks too much. She is seen as an inadequate mother here as she has been blind to Eric's drinking problems. However, she does not learn from these revelations and, at the end of the play, Sheila is worried that her parents are behaving as if nothing has happened and her mother asks **'Well, why shouldn't we?'** Mrs Birling has learned nothing from the Inspector and her complacent question shows her arrogant presumption that she can return to her old life without any further responsibility.

 ## Explore whether Sybil Birling is a terrible person

Sybil Birling is not a 2D cartoon villain. The audience is given a sense of a real closeness and affection between Sybil and Sheila at the start as they are united in their excitement of the engagement. We should also remember that Mrs Birling is a product of her time; brought up in a wealthy family during the Victorian era, she would have been instilled with a sense of innate snobbery, and her parenting of Eric and Sheila would have been defined by this upbringing. She also, tellingly, says to Sheila that Sheila will have to allow Gerald to work long hours away from her: **'you'll have to get used to that, just as I had'**. In 1912 British society, women's lives were restricted to the domestic sphere; it is no wonder she is narrow-minded, snobbish and petty. Yet, even with this background, it is hard to see her behaviour as anything other than inexcusable. Her own position in society is incredibly privileged and she abuses this by turning down Eva's desperate last plea for help. She knew Eva had nowhere else to turn but still refused her help, based on her prejudices and her snobbish pride. The Inspector tells us several times that Eva died a violent death, drinking disinfectant that **'burnt her inside out'** to remind us of the direct consequences of Sybil Birling's snobbery. She is a detestable character that the audience finds hard to empathise with.

Essential Exam Tips

- ☑ Try to embed quotations in your answer.

- ☑ Spend 5 minutes planning your answer; this helps you organise your ideas into a structure that is clear for the examiner.

4 Sheila Birling
Character analysis

Sheila is the Birling's daughter who begins the novel celebrating her engagement to Gerald Croft. The events throughout the play change her dramatically.

'when you never came near me, and I wondered what had happened to you'

- Despite the happiness of the engagement, Sheila refers to the summer when Gerald had been inexplicably distant.

- Even at the opening of the play, we see hints of underlying deceit and hypocrisy in the relationships. Sheila does not fully trust her fiance. Priestley **foreshadows** the confrontations that will soon explode in the Birling household.

'Oh- it's wonderful! Look- Mummy- isn't it a beauty?'

- Sheila is excited about her engagement ring, showing it to her mother.

- She is clearly delighted with it. Her **fragmented speech**, indicated through the dashes, shows her great excitement.

- She calls her mother **'mummy'**. The childish address shows her immaturity.

- She warms to Gerald, forgetting about the tension caused by his evasion about his distance in the summer. She comes across as shallow as she is so easily won over by a sparkling expensive ring.

There were limited options for employment and education for women in 1912 and women were expected to marry and bring up children. Sheila might be shallow in her excitement over the ring but she is restricted by the time period in which she lives and, by the standards of her society, she has achieved highly by securing a wealthy, aristocratic husband. Her excitement is understandable.

'I felt rotten about it at the time'

- Sheila admits to feeling guilty about her treatment of Eva Smith. She had Eva sacked from her job as sales girl in a temper caused by vanity and jealousy. Unlike her father, Sheila does admit to bad temper and poor judgement.

- Out of all the Birlings, her 'crime' against Eva was the most unjustifiable, based entirely on spite.

- The word **'rotten'** reflects her upper-class way of speaking, reminding us that she is in a position of power which she has abused.

- It is interesting that she says that she felt awful **'at the time'** which implies that the guilt did not last. Her sense of responsibility has since faded and she is still selfish at this point in the play.

There were almost no workers' rights in 1912. Sheila would have known that Eva would have been very vulnerable and there would be no opportunity for her to defend herself.

Priestley drew upon conventions of morality plays. These were plays performed in the Middle Ages which taught audiences how to behave through the repentance of the deadly sins. Sheila represents the deadly sin of envy.

(with sudden alarm) 'Mother- stop - stop!'

- As Mrs Birling begins to unknowingly condemn her own son at the end of Act 2, Sheila tries to stop her.

- The use of **'mother'** is different from the childish **'mummy'** that she uses at the start of the evening, showing that she is maturing.

- The *repeated* use of the *imperative verb* **'stop'** shows that Sheila is still interested in protecting her family rather than accepting the truth.

- Priestley uses Sheila as a *plot device* to heighten the dramatic tension at this point in the play. Her panic over her desire to stop her mother is infectious.

(bitterly) 'I suppose we're all nice people now'

- Sheila's ironic *tone* shows just how much she has changed from the beginning of the play as she is fully aware that the actions of herself and her family were unjustifiable.

- Her view of herself and her family has dramatically shifted and she cannot go back to the bubble of self-satisfied ignorance. The *stage direction* **'bitterly'** shows how disillusioned she has become.

- At the end of Act 3, Sheila remembers the Inspector's warning and is worried at how her parents have been unaffected by the evening's events.

- Sheila, as part of the younger generation, is a **symbol** of hope for the future; she has changed from the beginning of the play and is now aware that society also needs to change. The Inspector has the greatest impact on her.

- She **repeats** the Inspector's warning words, reminding the audience of his dark predictions about what will happen if society does not change. The **syndetic list** of destructive **nouns** reminds the audience of the horror that will be shortly enfolding.

The First World War was, in the eyes of the socialist Priestley, a consequence of the capitalist system that defined European society in the early 20th century. The economic rivalries between Germany, France and Great Britain helped pave the path to war, and so Sheila's anxiety over her parents' refusal to take responsibility for the poor in society is justified. It will be her generation which will be most affected by the two world wars that are coming.

 Grade 9 Exploration: Look at the character in a different way

How is structure used to show the transformation of Sheila?

At the start, Sheila is seen as self-satisfied with the **stage direction 'very pleased with life'**. However, there is, perhaps, already hope for change, as she tells Eric that **'You're squiffy'**. She is confrontational and uses a modern word **'squiffy'** which startles her mother, revealing that, as a young woman, she is picking up new ideas. Unlike her parents, she challenges Eric's drinking and in that, Priestley hints from the beginning that she might be different to the older generation and more susceptible to change. As the play progresses, Priestley shows in the **rising action** how Sheila had an encounter with Eva which left her with a guilty conscience and by the end of Act 1, it is Sheila alone who understands that the Inspector will change everything as she says to the evasive Gerald **'why – you fool – he knows. Of course he knows.'** Her increasing awareness heightens the audience's understanding of the Inspector's investigation and, by Act 3, her painful realisation of the flaws in society **contrasts** sharply with her parents' attitudes.

Priestley used the three unities of classical Greek theatre: unity of action, unity of time and unity of place. This means that the story unfolds in real time with no gaps; the effect of this is that the audience witnesses the transformation of Sheila live onstage.

She calls her mother **'mummy'**, showing her immaturity; her delight in the ring suggests that she is shallow.

Sheila admits to feeling guilty about her treatment of Eva, showing that she is beginning to develop a sense of social responsibility.

'Oh- it's wonderful! Look- Mummy- isn't it a beauty?'

'I felt rotten about it at the time'

Sheila begins the play as a shallow, immature girl.

Sheila changes throughout the play.

Sheila Birling

Sheila is most affected by the Inspector's revelations.

How is structure used to show the transformation of Sheila?

'fire and blood and anguish. And it frightens me the way you talk'

Even at the start, Sheila shows there is hope for change as, unlike her parents, she challenges Eric's drinking.

She refuses to go back to the old ways, and understands there are terrible consequences to a refusal to accept social responsibility.

Priestley uses the three unities of Greek theatre so that we see every step of Sheila's transformation live on stage.

Sample GCSE Exam Question & Answer

Q: Write about Sheila and the way that she is presented in the play.

☑ Make the point that Sheila begins the play as a girl celebrating her engagement

The play opens with the celebration of Sheila's engagement to Gerald, and Sheila is established as a young girl delighted with her life. She is excited about her engagement ring, showing it to her mother and exclaiming **'Oh- it's wonderful! Look- Mummy- isn't it a beauty?'** She is clearly thrilled with it, with the *fragmented speech*, indicated through the *dashes*, showing her great excitement. Her immaturity is seen in the childish address **'mummy'** and this immaturity is also evident as the presentation of the ring makes Sheila forget about how Gerald had been mysteriously absent earlier that year. She warms to Gerald, forgetting about the tension caused by his evasion about his distance in the summer. She comes across as shallow as she is so easily won over by a sparkling expensive ring. Yet we should remember that there were limited options for employment and education for women in 1912 and women were expected to marry and bring up children. Sheila might be shallow in her excitement over the ring but she is restricted by the time period in which she lives and, by the standards of her society, she has achieved highly by securing a wealthy, aristocratic husband. Her excitement is understandable.

☑ Move on to the point that Sheila is presented as someone who is spiteful and jealous

Later on, Sheila admits to feeling guilty about her treatment of Eva Smith. She had Eva sacked from her job as sales girl in a fit of temper caused by vanity and jealousy because Eva looked prettier in a dress than she did. When questioned by the Inspector, she tells the story and confesses that **'I felt rotten about it at the time'**. Unlike her father, Sheila does own up to bad temper and poor judgement yet it is interesting that she says that she felt awful **'at the time'** which implies that the guilt did not last. Her sense of responsibility that she felt afterwards has since faded and she is still selfish at this point in the play. The word **'rotten'** reflects her upper-class way of speaking, reminding us that she is in a position of power which she abused; there were almost no workers' rights in 1912 and Sheila would have known that Eva would have been very vulnerable and there would be no opportunity for her to defend herself. Indeed, out of all the Birlings, her 'crime' against Eva was the most unjustifiable, based entirely on spite. Priestley drew upon conventions of morality play which were plays performed in the Middle Ages which taught audiences how to behave through the repentance of the deadly sins; through the incident of the dress, Sheila represents the deadly sin of envy.

☑ Make the point that Sheila does begin to change throughout the play

Yet Sheila is able to acknowledge her mistake and is able to change. Indeed, the play's structure reflects her transformation and even from the beginning, Sheila shows how she has the potential to alter her attitudes as she tells Eric that **'You're squiffy'**. She is confrontational and uses a modern word **'squiffy'** which startles her mother, revealing that, as a young woman, she is picking up new ideas. Unlike her parents, she challenges Eric's drinking and in that, Priestley hints from the beginning that she might be different to the older generation and more susceptible to reform. This ability to change brings hope and Sheila does indeed respond to the Inspector's revelations so that by the end of Act 1, it is Sheila alone who understands that the Inspector will change everything as she says to the evasive Gerald **'why – you fool – he knows. Of course he knows.'** Her increasing awareness heightens the audience's understanding of the Inspector's investigation and, by Act 3, her painful realisation of the flaws in society contrasts sharply with her parents' blinkered attitude. Priestley uses the three unities of classical Greek theatre: unity of action, unity of time and unity of place. This means that the story unfolds in real time with no gaps; the effect of this is that the audience witnesses the transformation of Sheila live onstage. Priestley ensures that her emotional journey is gripping for the audience as she is trapped between her loyalty to her family and her newfound social responsibility. An example of this is when Mrs Birling begins to unknowingly condemn her own son at the end of Act 2 and Sheila tries to stop her, calling out **(with sudden alarm) 'Mother- stop - stop!'** The use of **'mother'** is different from the childish **'mummy'** that she uses at the start of the evening, showing that she is maturing, but the *repeated* use of the *imperative verb* **'stop'** indicates that Sheila is still interested in protecting her family rather than accepting the truth. Priestley uses Sheila as a ***plot device*** to heighten the dramatic tension at this point in the play as her panic over her desire to stop her mother and save her brother is infectious.

☑ Move to the end of the play and establish how Sheila has changed

By Act 3, the audience can see a very different girl to the one at the start as Sheila says **(bitterly) I suppose we're all nice people now'**. Her ironic *tone* shows just how much she has changed from the beginning of the play as she is now fully aware that the actions of herself and her family were unjustifiable. Her view of herself and her family has been dramatically shifted and she cannot go back to the bubble of self-satisfied ignorance. The ***stage direction* 'bitterly'** shows how disillusioned she has become. This disillusionment is mixed with anxiety. Sheila remembers the Inspector's warning and is worried at how her parents have been unaffected by the evening's events as she states **'Fire and blood and anguish. And it frightens me the way you talk'**. She *repeats* the Inspector's warning words, reminding the audience of his dark predictions about what will happen if society does not change. The *syndetic list* of destructive *nouns* reminds the audience of the horror that will be shortly unfolding. The First World War was, in the eyes of the socialist Priestley, a consequence of the capitalist system that defined European society in the early 20th century. The economic rivalries between Germany, France and Great Britain helped pave the path to war, and so Sheila's anxiety over her parents' refusal to take responsibility for the poor in society is justified. It will be her generation which will be most affected by the two world wars that are coming. Sheila, as part of the younger generation, is a *symbol* of hope for the future; the Inspector has the greatest impact on her and she has changed dramatically from the beginning of the play and is now aware that society also needs to change.

Essential Exam Tips

- ☑ Leave time for checking through your work. One tip is to check each paragraph as you finish it before starting the next one.

- ☑ You don't need to learn exactly what happens in each act. Referring to 'the opening'/'when the Inspector leaves' etc is fine.

5 Eric Birling
Character analysis

Eric is the shy, uncomfortable son of the Birlings who is exposed as a man who abused Eva Smith and stole money from the family business. Like his sister Sheila, he shows guilt and remorse for his actions.

'You're squiffy'

- In Act 1, Sheila states very clearly that Eric is **'squiffy'** after Eric laughs and then quickly suppresses this laugh.

- He is a young man who is drinking too heavily and this excessive drinking immediately suggests to the audience that he is a weak character.

- It could be that he is drinking because he has been badly parented; certainly, his parents seem blind to his drinking. It could be that his drinking is a result of being dismissed by his father, who seems to find him irritating and excludes him from conversations.

- Eric's heavy drinking establishes tension from the beginning of the play; Priestley uses his drunken laugh as an early indication that the Birlings' apparent security and pleasure in life is a facade.

British society in 1912 was strictly controlled with a rigid hierarchy of social class. Eric is a young man who has been incredibly privileged by being born into a wealthy family which has paid for his university education and provided a job in the family firm. This was to ensure that the wealth and power stayed in the family but Eric's excessive drinking is Priestley's way of showing that this family retention of wealth is unhealthy.

'Why shouldn't they try for higher wages? We try for the highest possible prices.'

- In Act 1, Eric approves of Eva's attempt to secure a pay rise, telling his father that Eva was justified in asking for better wages.

- Eric has a different, more equitable (fair) attitude to the workers than his father has.

Capitalism was the economic system which shaped society in 1912. Capitalism meant that rich landowners and factory owners were able to control the labour force, resulting in profit for those in control but often poor living and working conditions for the workers. Priestley was a socialist and believed in a fairer distribution of resources, and Eric's reasonable query reflects Priestley's attitudes.

'I was in that state when a chap easily turns nasty' 'used her... as if she was an animal, a thing, not a person'

- Eric admits that he forced himself into Daisy's house and also forced her to have sex, as he was drunk and on the verge of violence.

- He openly admits his guilt here and his confession shows honesty. Yet he uses the *noun* **'chap'** to describe himself; it has the effect of making him sound jolly and rather harmless, as if he is trying to excuse his actions.

- Later, the Inspector tells him clearly that his behaviour was disgusting, that Eric treated Daisy **'as if she was an animal, a thing, not a person'**. The *list* shows how Eric abused his position as a rich man of great privilege by diminishing a lonely, poor girl and seeing her as sub-human- an **'animal'** and even an object - **'a thing'**.

As a poor girl in 1912, Daisy would have been in a vulnerable position and it would have been easy for the wealthy Eric to take advantage of this. Priestley drew upon conventions of morality plays. These were plays performed in the Middle Ages which taught audiences how to behave through repentance of the deadly sins. Eric represents the deadly sin of lust.

'I've got to cover this up as soon as I can. You damned fool-'

- Eric confesses to stealing and his father's response is to **'cover this up'** rather than address or resolve it.

- Eric is exposed to his family and the audience as a thief.

- There is evidence that Mr Birling has parented Eric badly. He snaps at Eric that he is a **'damned fool'**; this insult is patronising and vicious, and shows how Mr Birling despises his son. He makes little effort to understand Eric's actions and instead verbally attacks him, showing himself to be an inadequate father. The audience might well sympathise with Eric at this point.

> (shouting) 'And I say the girl's dead and we all helped to kill her- and that's what matters-'

- By the end of Act 3, Eric has changed from the unconfident boy we see in Act 1; here he admits that he killed Eva, blames his family as well and dismisses his father's concerns over public exposure.

- The *stage direction* shows his great passion; earlier in the play he was easily silenced but here he is **'shouting'**, reflecting his desire to be heard and to challenge his family.

- His *declarative statement* **'we all helped to kill her'** clearly states that they are guilty. The *inclusive pronoun* **'we'** means that no one is allowed to excuse themselves from their actions.

> The First World War was, in the eyes of the socialist Priestley, a consequence of the capitalist system that defined European society in the early 20th century. The economic rivalries between Germany, France and Great Britain helped pave the path to war, and so Eric's anxiety over his parents' refusal to take responsibility for the poor in society is justified. It will be his generation which will be most affected by the two world wars that are coming.

 Grade 9 Exploration: Look at the character in a different way

Is Eric a symbol of hope at the end of the play?

Yes: Eric, as part of the younger generation, is a *symbol* of hope for the future; he has changed from the beginning of the play and is now aware that society also needs to change. He refuses to copy his parents in ignoring the evening's revelations, saying **'You lot may be letting yourselves out nicely, but I can't'**. The *modal verb* **'can't'** shows an emphatic choice to accept his share of responsibility that *contrasts* sharply with his parents and bodes well for the future.

No: His immaturity in Act 3 is still clear in the *stage direction* **'sulkily'** which is *repeated* twice. This *adverb* reaffirms his boyish attitude. He is constantly led by the stronger, more vocal Sheila, echoing her words; it is Sheila, with her refusal to take back Gerald's ring and therefore simply revert to the beginning of the play, who is the one who really is a *symbol* of hope for the audience.

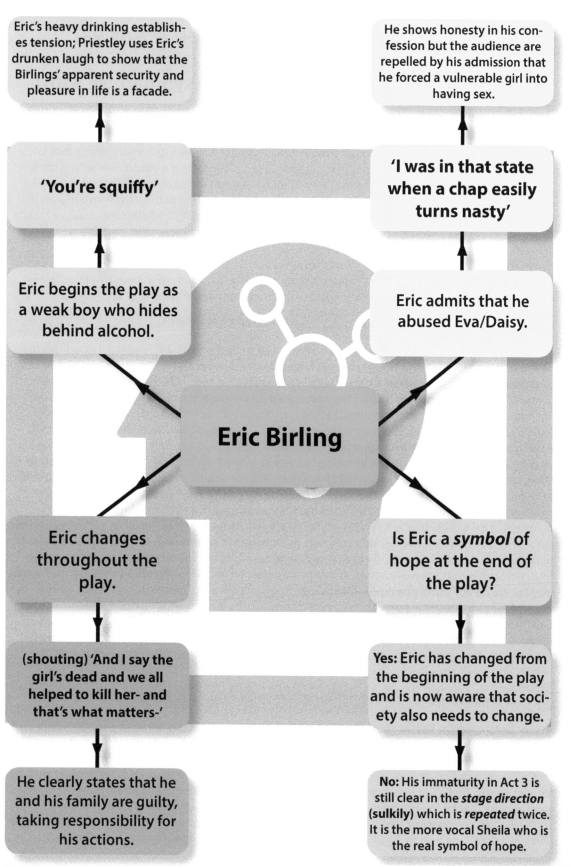

Eric's heavy drinking establishes tension; Priestley uses Eric's drunken laugh to show that the Birlings' apparent security and pleasure in life is a facade.

He shows honesty in his confession but the audience are repelled by his admission that he forced a vulnerable girl into having sex.

'You're squiffy'

'I was in that state when a chap easily turns nasty'

Eric begins the play as a weak boy who hides behind alcohol.

Eric admits that he abused Eva/Daisy.

Eric Birling

Eric changes throughout the play.

Is Eric a *symbol* of hope at the end of the play?

(shouting) 'And I say the girl's dead and we all helped to kill her- and that's what matters-'

Yes: Eric has changed from the beginning of the play and is now aware that society also needs to change.

He clearly states that he and his family are guilty, taking responsibility for his actions.

No: His immaturity in Act 3 is still clear in the *stage direction* (sulkily) which is *repeated* twice. It is the more vocal Sheila who is the real symbol of hope.

Sample GCSE Exam Question & Answer

Q: Is Eric a character that audiences can sympathise with?

☑ Make the point that Eric is established as a young man who drinks heavily

Eric is established from the beginning as a heavy drinker. In Act 1, Sheila states very clearly that Eric is **'squiffy'** after Eric laughs and then quickly suppresses this laugh. He is a young man who is drinking too heavily and this excessive drinking immediately suggests to the audience that he is a weak character. Eric's heavy drinking establishes tension from the beginning of the play; Priestley uses his drunken laugh as an early indication that the Birlings' apparent security and pleasure in life is a facade. British society in 1912 was strictly controlled with a rigid hierarchy of social class, and Eric is a young man who has been incredibly privileged by being born into a wealthy family which has paid for his university education and provided a job in the family firm. This was to ensure that the wealth and power stayed in the family but Eric's excessive drinking is Priestley's way of showing that this family retention of wealth is unhealthy. Eric's initial presentation is not a positive one to the audience.

☑ Develop the point that Eric is an unattractive character

As the play develops, much more unpleasant aspects of Eric's character are revealed. Eric admits that he forced himself into Daisy's house and also forced her to have sex, as he was drunk and on the verge of violence: **'in that state when a chap easily turns nasty'**. He openly admits his guilt here and his confession shows honesty yet he uses the *noun* **'chap'** to describe himself; it has the effect of making him sound jolly and rather harmless, as if he is trying to excuse his actions. Later, the Inspector tells him clearly that his behaviour was disgusting, that Eric treated Daisy **'as if she was an animal, a thing, not a person'**. The *list* shows how Eric abused his position as a rich man of great privilege by diminishing a lonely, poor girl and seeing her as sub-human- an **'animal'** and even an object - **'a thing'**. As a poor girl in 1912, Daisy would have been in a vulnerable position and it would have been easy for the wealthy Eric to take advantage of this. Priestley drew upon conventions of morality plays which were plays performed in the Middle Ages that taught audiences how to behave through repentance of the deadly sins. Eric represents the deadly sin of lust however, he is not a complete monster. The audience sees a warmer side to him as he does form a relationship of sorts with Daisy after that night. He also shows humanity in Act 1 when he approves of Eva's attempt to secure a pay rise, telling his father that Eva was justified in asking for better wages: **'Why shouldn't they try for higher wages? We try for the highest possible prices.'** Eric has a different, more equitable (fair) attitude to the workers than his father has. Capitalism was the economic system which shaped society in 1912. Capitalism meant that rich landowners and factory owners were able to control the labour force, resulting in profit for those in control but often poor living and working conditions for the workers. Priestley was a socialist and believed in a fairer distribution of resources, and Eric's reasonable query reflects Priestley's attitudes.

☑ Explore whether Eric's behaviour is a result of the way his parents treat him

Audience reactions to Eric can be influenced by the clear indications that he has been badly parented; certainly, his parents seem blind to his drinking. He also does not seem valued by his parents and it is possible that his drinking is a result of being dismissed by his father, who seems to find him irritating and excludes him from conversations. Later, when Eric confesses to stealing, his father's response is to **'cover this up'**. Mr Birling's instincts are simply to hide the issue rather than address or resolve it and this suggests that he has been a poor role model to him son. It is clear to the watching audience that Mr Birling has parented Eric badly. He snaps at Eric that he is a **'damned fool'**; this insult is patronising and vicious, and shows how Mr Birling despises his son. He makes little effort to understand Eric's actions and instead verbally attacks him, showing himself to be an inadequate father. The audience could easily sympathise with Eric at this point in the play.

☑ Move to the point that Eric does change throughout the play

By the end of Act 3, Eric has changed from the unconfident boy we see in Act 1, **(shouting) And I say the girl's dead and we all helped to kill her- and that's what matters-'**. Here he admits that he killed Eva, blames his family as well and dismisses his father's concerns over public exposure. The ***stage direction*** shows his great passion; earlier in the play he was easily silenced but here he is **'shouting'**, reflecting his desire to be heard and to challenge his family. His ***declarative statement*** **'we all helped kill her'** clearly states that they are guilty. The ***inclusive pronoun*** **'we'** means that no one is allowed to excuse themselves from their actions. The First World War was, in the eyes of the socialist Priestley, a consequence of the capitalist system that defined European society in the early 20th century. The economic rivalries between Germany, France and Great Britain helped pave the path to war, and so Eric's anxiety over his parents' refusal to take responsibility for the poor in society is justified. It will be his generation which will be most affected by the two world wars that are coming. Eric, as part of the younger generation, is a ***symbol*** of hope for the future; he has changed from the beginning of the play and is now aware that society also needs to change. He refuses to copy his parents in ignoring the evening's revelations, saying **'You lot may be letting yourselves out nicely, but I can't'**. The ***modal verb*** **'can't'** shows an emphatic choice to accept his share of responsibility that ***contrasts*** sharply with his parents and bodes well for the future. However, his immaturity in Act 3 is still clear in the ***stage direction*** **(sulkily)** which is ***repeated*** twice and this ***adverb*** reaffirms his boyish attitude. He is constantly led by the stronger, more vocal Sheila, echoing her words; it is Sheila, with her refusal to take back Gerald's ring and therefore simply revert to the beginning of the play, who is perhaps the one who really is a ***symbol*** of hope for the audience, not Eric.

Essential Exam Tips

☑ **When writing about themes, make sure you explain how the ideas affect the characters and also apply to the reader.**

☑ **Exam boards use different wording for the modern text literature question. Check with your teacher or the exam board's website to see what sort of question your board sets.**

6 Gerald Croft
Character analysis

Gerald Croft is the well-mannered, aristocratic young man who is celebrating his engagement to Sheila Birling. His secret relationship with Daisy Renton is exposed yet his reactions to the fall-out of the evening are complex.

'easy well-bred young man-about-town'

- The opening *stage direction* establishes Gerald as a confident, privileged man.

- The description that places him as a **'man-about-town'** suggests that he is worldly and sociable.

- His social position as **'well-bred'** means that his marriage to Sheila will improve the Birlings' status. The marriage will ally the two families closely together which will be good for business for both.

British society in 1912 was strictly controlled with a rigid hierarchy of social class. Gerald is a **'well-bred'** young man who has been incredibly privileged by being born into a wealthy family which has provided a job in the family firm.

'when you never came near me, and I wondered what had happened to you'

- Despite the happiness of the engagement, Sheila refers to the summer when Gerald had been inexplicably distant.

- Even at the opening of the play, we see hints of underlying deceit and hypocrisy in the relationships. Gerald is being established as a character who is untrustworthy. Priestley *foreshadows* the confrontations that will soon explode in the Birling household.

'young and fresh and charming'

- Gerald describes Daisy as **'young and fresh and charming'**.

- There is a rather unpleasant sense of a predator in the **syndetic list** which makes it clear that Gerald was attracted to Daisy's youth and physical looks.

> Priestley drew upon conventions of morality plays. These were plays performed in the Middle Ages which taught audiences how to behave through repentance of the deadly sins. Gerald Croft represents the deadly sin of lust.

(sharp sarcasm) 'You were the wonderful Fairy Prince'

- Sheila is bitter in her statement that Gerald was Daisy's flawed fairy-tale prince as he tells the story of how he rescued her from an unpleasant situation but then used her as his mistress.

- The **stage direction** 'sharp sarcasm' shows how disillusioned Sheila has become with her well-mannered fiance. The **tone** alerts the audience that Gerald has abused his position and that there was nothing **'wonderful'** about his behaviour.

> As a poor girl in 1912, Daisy/Eva would have been in a vulnerable position and it would have been easy for the wealthy Gerald to take advantage of this.

'As I'm rather more- upset... and- well, I'd like to be alone'

- Gerald is emotionally affected by the realisation that his ex-lover has committed suicide.

- The **fragmented speech** indicated by the **ellipsis** and **dashes** shows his agitation and grief.

- His obvious distress ensures that the audience sees another side to Gerald; he is not just a cold-hearted abuser of innocent women, but is a man who had an emotional connection with his lover.

- His desire to be alone means that he leaves the stage; Priestley here uses his exit as a **plot device** so that the Inspector is free to move on with his investigation.

- Gerald's last words of the play show his arrogance as he expects everything to return to normal and for Sheila to continue with their marriage plans.

- His question sounds off-hand and complacent. He has shrugged off the evening's revelations and is keen to resume his old life, unaffected by the events.

- He provides a ***contrast*** to the other young people, Sheila and Eric, who have been profoundly (significantly) affected by the Inspector's revelations.

> Gerald belonged to the aristocratic class which had a vested interest in maintaining the status quo. The First World War shattered this status quo, with 17% of the aristocratic officers being killed on the battlefields. Priestley wrote the play in 1945, the last year of the WW2; he was keen to ensure that society started afresh and did not revert to the old ways. Gerald's narrow-minded, complacent attitude jars with the post-war audience in his desire for Sheila to take back the ring.

 ## Grade 9 Exploration: Look at the character in a different way

<u>Is there any honour left in Gerald by the end of the play?</u>

Yes: At the end of the play, Gerald admits his mistake, saying **'I did keep a girl last summer. I've admitted it. And I'm sorry, Sheila'**. The simple, ***declarative sentences*** reveal an openness and honesty that was missing from his character at the start of the play. He also gives a genuine, heartfelt apology to Sheila which shows a respect for her and their relationship. With this honest communication, there seems to be a sense of honour left in Gerald and therefore hope for his future with Sheila.

No: Gerald's admission here is dismissive, with the simple statements suggesting an impatience and lack of any need for a full explanation. He refers to the dead Daisy as just **'a girl'**. The ***determiner*** **'a'** shows that he is not really thinking of Daisy, his dead lover, as anyone significant. He has moved on with almost obscene haste from his earlier grief and remorse. At the end of the play, he does not even give Daisy her name, showing his callous disregard for his dead mistress. Gerald ends the play a diminished, unlikeable character.

He is a confident young man and, because he is 'well-bred', he is an excellent match for Sheila.

↑

'Easy well-bred young man-about-town'

↑

Gerald is a wealthy member of the aristocracy.

Gerald Croft

Sheila's sarcasm shows the audience how Gerald's behaviour was despicable; he took advantage of a vulnerable girl and cast her aside when he became bored of the relationship.

↑

(sharp sarcasm) 'You were the wonderful Fairy Prince'

↑

Gerald has an affair with Daisy.

Gerald does not learn to take responsibility.

↓

'What about this ring?'

↓

He is keen to bury the evening's revelations and revert back to the beginning of the play.

Is there any honour left in Gerald by the end of the play?

↓

Yes: Gerald admits his relationship with Daisy and apologises, showing an honesty that was missing at the start.

↓

No: Gerald dismisses Daisy as 'a girl'. The *determiner* 'a' shows that he is not really thinking of his dead lover as anyone significant and is callously moving on.

Sample GCSE Exam Question & Answer

Q: How is Gerald presented in the play?

☑ Make the point that Gerald is presented as a member of the aristocratic class

Gerald Croft is the well-mannered, aristocratic young man who is celebrating his engagement to Sheila Birling. The opening **stage direction** establishes Gerald as an '**easy well-bred young man-about-town**'. The description that places him as a '**man about town**' suggests that he is worldly and sociable; the class he has been born into in 1912 has allowed him the education and opportunities to move freely in society. The fact that he is '**well-bred**' means that he is viewed as an excellent match for Sheila, and indeed, their relationship does seem to have hints of financial transaction as their marriage will link the Crofts and Birlings more closely together in business. However, despite the surface happiness of the engagement, Sheila refers to the summer when Gerald had been inexplicably distant: '**when you never came near me, and I wondered what had happened to you**'. Even at the opening of the play, we see hints of underlying deceit and hypocrisy in the relationships. Gerald is being established as a character who is untrustworthy as Priestley **foreshadows** the confrontations that will soon explode in the Birling household.

☑ Develop this point that Gerald abuses his privileged position

Gerald is incredibly privileged yet he abuses this position with his treatment of Daisy Renton. He describes Daisy as '**young and fresh and charming**'. There is a rather unpleasant sense of a predator in the **syndetic list** which makes it clear that Gerald was attracted to Daisy's youth and physical looks. Priestley drew upon conventions of morality plays which were plays performed in the Middle Ages that taught audiences how to behave through repentance of the deadly sins; Gerald Croft represents the deadly sin of lust and this is clear in his description of Daisy. The audience is further alienated from him through Sheila's bitter reaction as she says, with (**sharp sarcasm**) '**You were the wonderful Fairy Prince**'. Gerald was Daisy's flawed fairy-tale prince as he tells the story of how he rescued her from an unpleasant situation but then used her as his mistress. The **stage direction** '**sharp sarcasm**' shows how disillusioned Sheila has become with her well-mannered fiance and how their relationship is crumbling. The **tone** also alerts the audience that Gerald has abused his position and that there was nothing '**wonderful**' about his behaviour. As a poor girl in 1912, Daisy/Eva would have been in a vulnerable position and it would have been easy for the wealthy Gerald to take advantage of this.

☑ Move to the point that Gerald is a character who is affected by the revelations

Gerald is emotionally affected by the realisation that his ex-lover has committed suicide, saying '**as I'm rather more- upset…. and- well, I'd like to be alone**'. The **fragmented speech** indicated by the **ellipsis** and **dashes** shows his agitation and grief. The events also seem to have changed Gerald; he admits his mistake in Act 3, saying '**I did keep a girl last summer. I've admitted it. And I'm sorry, Sheila**'. The simple, **declarative sentences** reveal an openness and honesty that was missing from his character at the start of the play. He also gives a genuine, heartfelt apology to Sheila which shows a respect for her and their relationship. With this honest communication, there seems to be a sense of honour left in Gerald and therefore hope for his future with Sheila. Yet this is only one interpretation and it could be argued that Gerald is left without any honour at the play. Gerald's admission here is dismissive, with the simple statements suggesting an impatience and lack of any need for a full explanation. He refers to the dead Daisy as just '**a girl**'. The **determiner** '**a**' shows that he is not really thinking of Daisy, his dead lover, as anyone significant. He has moved on with almost obscene haste from his earlier grief and remorse. At the end of the play, he does not even give Daisy her name, showing his callous disregard for his dead mistress.

☑ Develop the point that Gerald is presented negatively at the end of the play

Gerald's last words of the play show his arrogance - **'What about this ring?'** - as he expects everything to return to normal and for Sheila to continue with their marriage plans. The ring is a *symbol* of his love for her but it also *symbolic* of his possession of her, reflecting again the idea of their marriage being based on business considerations. His question sounds off-hand and complacent, showing how he has shrugged off the horror of the evening's revelations and is keen to resume his old life, unaffected by the events. Gerald belonged to the aristocratic class which had a vested interest in maintaining the status quo. The First World War shattered this status quo, with 17% of the aristocratic officers being killed on the battlefields. Priestley wrote the play in 1945, the last year of the Second World War; he was keen to ensure that society started afresh and did not revert to the old ways. Gerald's narrow-minded, complacent attitude jars with the audience in his desire for Sheila to take back the ring, bury the evening's revelations and return to their previous relationship as if nothing had happened. Gerald ends the play a diminished, unlikeable character, and it is Sheila that the audience looks to as a beacon of hope for change within society.

Essential Exam Tips

☑ Look for powerful language: interesting adverbs, imperative verbs, passionate similes etc. If you can use the correct literary terminology, do!

☑ Don't just label a quotation as a 'simile' or 'verb' etc. Explain the effect of the language: what it shows about a character or a theme and how the reader's response is affected by the language.

7 Eva Smith/Daisy Renton
Character analysis

We never see on stage the character of Eva/Daisy but she dominates the play. Her suicide is investigated by the Inspector and the involvement of the Birlings and the Crofts in her life is revealed in a dramatic and damning way.

'Burnt her inside out, of course'

- The audience first hears about Eva Smith through the Inspector who tells the Birlings that there has been an incident which involved Eva swallowing disinfectant which **'burnt her inside out, of course'**.

- The graphic **vocabulary** of the corrosive liquid destroying Eva's body is shocking to the Birlings and also to the audience. The matter-of-fact **interjection** 'of course' only highlights just how appalling her death was; there was no doubt at all about the fatal outcome of her actions.

> By establishing the crime, Priestley follows the formula for a classic whodunnit, a detective story where the audience has to guess who the criminal is. However, the whodunnit is not the definitive genre; 'An Inspector Calls' could fit into the genre of a morality play, a political play or a drama about family life.

'She'd had a lot to say- far too much'

- Mr Birling describes Eva as the articulate ringleader of a group of workers who asked for a wage increase.

- The added comment **'far too much'** suggests Mr Birling's disapproval of Eva's vocal requests. Yet the audience already distrusts Mr Birling's opinions and so we admire the courage of this woman who dared to challenge the employer who kept her wages low.

> 1912 was a year of strikes and labour unrest, and Eva's involvement in the strike at Birling's factory reflects contemporary events. Priestley was a socialist and wanted to see society change so that there was a fairer distribution of profit and that workers like Eva were treated more fairly. Through Mr Birling's arrogant disapproval of Eva, we see Priestley criticise the capitalist system.

'no work, no money coming in, and living in lodgings, with no relatives to help her'

- The Inspector describes how Eva/Daisy was alone and poor.

- The dense *repetition* of the *determiner* **'no'** reminds the Birlings and the audience how Daisy was isolated and very vulnerable which arouses our pity.

- The word **'lodgings'** suggests temporary, bleak accommodation which *contrasts* with the **'good solid furniture'** that are used in the opening *stage directions* to show the prosperity and security of the Birlings.

'young and fresh and charming'

- Gerald describes Eva/Daisy as **'young and fresh and charming'**.

- There is a rather unpleasant sense of a predator in the *syndetic list* which makes it clear that Gerald was attracted to Eva/Daisy's youth and physical looks.

Priestley drew upon conventions of morality plays. These were plays performed in the Middle Ages which taught audiences how to behave through repentance of the deadly sins. Gerald Croft represents the deadly sin of lust.

'girls of that class'

- Mrs Birling dismisses Eva Smith as **'girls of that class'**.

- Eva is seen as just one of many working girls. By grouping the girls together, Mrs Birling reflects the common contemporary view that saw the workers as a type, not as individuals. She distances herself from women of a class that is different to hers.

Society in 1912 was strictly controlled with a rigid hierarchy of social class. We see the isolation of Eva and the lack of respect given to her by the upper classes.

- After Gerald ended their relationship, Daisy went away to be by herself.
- There is a sense of sadness and reflection in the *anaphora*. We see that the affair meant a lot to her and that she is a girl hurt from the rejection of a failed love.

'As if a girl of that sort would ever refuse money!'

- Mrs Birling laughs at the idea of Daisy turning down the stolen money from Eric, yet this is exactly what Daisy did.
- Daisy is shown as a girl of strong morals, refusing to accept the money which came from crime. She is seen as morally superior to the Birlings and Crofts, with an integrity (honesty) that they lack.

Priestley challenges the rigid class system which assumed that those born into a high class were 'better' than the working class.

 ## Grade 9 Exploration: Look at the character in a different way

Is Eva a symbol or a real character?

Symbol: Eva is used as a *symbol* by Priestley to represent the poor and vulnerable in society. She is an *everyman* character who the audience can identify with. The Inspector tells us that, beyond the story of the girl in the mortuary, there are still **'millions and millions and millions of Eva Smiths'** to be considered and to take responsibility for. The lack of presence of Eva on the stage contributes to this sense that she is merely a *symbol* of the working class women.

Real character: The physical details are relayed to us through all of the characters to build up a potent visual picture of her; we know she is **'twenty-four... very pretty'** and we also learn a lot about her strong, compelling personality so that we keenly feel the tragedy of her death.

Some productions, including the BBC TV adaptation of the play, have flash-backs showing Eva as a character interacting with the Birlings. These certainly help to make her seem more a of 'real' character yet, even completely removed from the stage, Eva dominates the play.

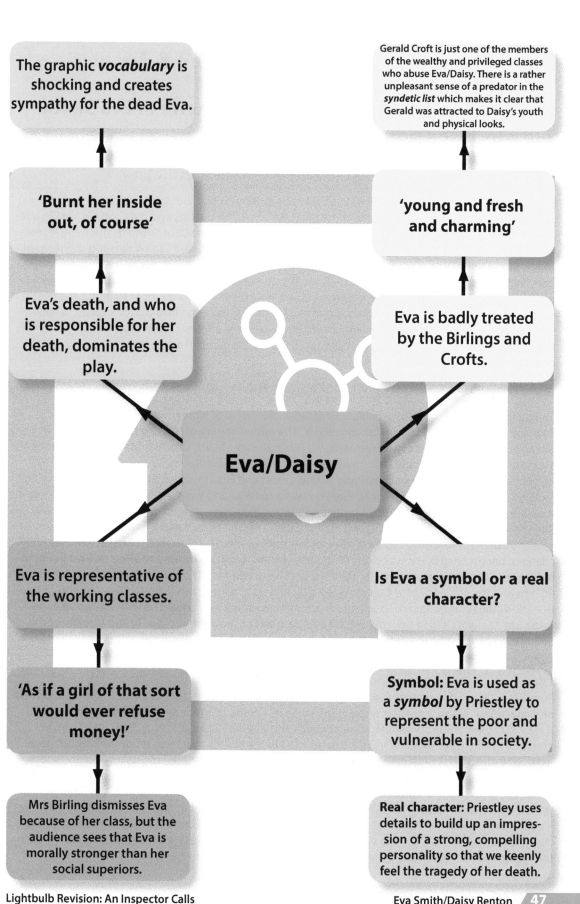

The graphic *vocabulary* is shocking and creates sympathy for the dead Eva.

Gerald Croft is just one of the members of the wealthy and privileged classes who abuse Eva/Daisy. There is a rather unpleasant sense of a predator in the *syndetic list* which makes it clear that Gerald was attracted to Daisy's youth and physical looks.

'Burnt her inside out, of course'

'young and fresh and charming'

Eva's death, and who is responsible for her death, dominates the play.

Eva is badly treated by the Birlings and Crofts.

Eva/Daisy

Eva is representative of the working classes.

Is Eva a symbol or a real character?

'As if a girl of that sort would ever refuse money!'

Symbol: Eva is used as a *symbol* by Priestley to represent the poor and vulnerable in society.

Mrs Birling dismisses Eva because of her class, but the audience sees that Eva is morally stronger than her social superiors.

Real character: Priestley uses details to build up an impression of a strong, compelling personality so that we keenly feel the tragedy of her death.

Sample GCSE Exam Question & Answer

Q: How does Priestley present the character of Eva Smith and why is she significant in the play?

☑ Make the point that Eva is a character who dominates the play

We never see on stage the character of Eva Smith/Daisy Renton but she dominates the play. Her suicide is investigated by the Inspector and the involvement of the Birlings and the Crofts in her life is revealed in a dramatic and damning way. The audience first hears about Eva Smith through the Inspector who tells the Birlings that there has been an incident which involved Eva swallowing disinfectant which **'burnt her inside out, of course'**. The graphic *vocabulary* of the corrosive liquid destroying Eva's body is shocking to the Birlings and also to the audience. The matter-of-fact *interjection* **'of course'** only highlights just how appalling her death was; there was no doubt at all about the fatal outcome of her actions. By establishing the crime, Priestley follows the formula for a classic whodunnit, a detective story where the audience has to guess who the criminal is. However, the whodunnit is not the definitive genre; 'An Inspector Calls' could fit into the genre of a morality play, a political play or a drama about family life.

☑ Move to the point that she is presented as a sympathetic character

Mr Birling describes Eva as the articulate ringleader of a group of workers who asked for a wage increase: **'She'd had a lot to say- far too much'**. The added comment **'far too much'** suggests Mr Birling's disapproval of Eva's vocal requests. Yet the audience already distrusts Mr Birling's opinions and so we admire the courage of this woman who dared to challenge the employer who kept her wages low. 1912 was a year of strikes and labour unrest and Eva's involvement in the strike at Birling's factory reflects contemporary events. Priestley was a socialist and wanted to see society change so that there was a fairer distribution of profit and that workers were treated more fairly. Through Mr Birling's arrogant disapproval of Eva, we see Priestley criticise the capitalist system. Later, Priestley uses the Inspector to arouse our sympathy for her through his description of how Eva, who has changed her name to Daisy, was alone and poor with **'no work, no money coming in, and living in lodgings, with no relatives to help her'**. The dense *repetition* of the *determiner* **'no'** reminds the Birlings and the audience how Daisy was isolated and very vulnerable which arouses our pity. The word **'lodgings'** suggests temporary, bleak accommodation which *contrasts* with the **'good solid furniture'** that are used in the opening *stage directions* to show the prosperity and security of the Birlings.

☑ Move to the point that Eva/Daisy is seen as a victim

Priestley consistently presents Eva/Daisy to us as a victim. Gerald describes Daisy as **'young and fresh and charming'**. There is a rather unpleasant sense of a predator in the *syndetic list* which makes it clear that Gerald was attracted to Daisy's youth and physical looks. Priestley drew upon conventions of morality plays which were plays performed in the Middle Ages that taught audiences how to behave through repentance of the deadly sins. Gerald Croft represents the deadly sin of lust. She is also victimised by the other Birlings; indeed, Mrs Birling completely dismisses her as **'girls of that class'**. Eva is seen as just one of many working girls. By grouping the girls together, Mrs Birling reflects the common contemporary view that saw the workers as a type, not as individuals, and she distances herself from women of a class that is different to hers. Society in 1912 was strictly controlled with a rigid hierarchy of social class and we see the isolation of Eva and the lack of respect given to her by the upper classes. This directs the audience to empathise with Eva rather than the Birlings.

☑ Explore how far Eva/Daisy is a symbol rather than a real character

Eva is used as a **symbol** by Priestley to represent the poor and vulnerable in society, as an **every-man** character. The Inspector tells us that, beyond the story of the girl in the mortuary, there are still **'millions and millions and millions of Eva Smiths'** to be considered and to take responsibility for. The lack of presence of Eva on the stage contributes to this sense that she is merely a **symbol** of the working class women. Yet she is also a real character. The physical details are relayed to us through all of the characters to build up a concrete picture of her; we know she is **'twenty-four... very pretty'** and we also learn a lot about her strong, compelling personality so that we keenly feel the tragedy of her death. Some productions, including the BBC TV adaptation of the play, have flashbacks showing Eva as a character interacting with the Birlings. These certainly help to make her seem more a of 'real' character yet, even completely removed from the stage, Eva dominates the play.

 ## Essential Exam Tips

☑ **Don't spend ages writing an introduction. Get stuck into the question straightaway.**

☑ **Keep an eye on the time. Write the time that you need to have finished this 'An Inspector Calls' question on a piece of paper and stick to it. If you run over too much, your response to the next question will suffer.**

'An Inspector Calls' is a play that is full of tension, with Priestley using many dramatic devices (techniques) to ensure that the audience is fully engaged.

'So long as we behave ourselves, don't get into the police court or start a scandal- eh?' (laughs complacently)

- **Foreshadowing** is used to create dramatic tension. Arthur Birling predicts that his knighthood is almost guaranteed.

- Priestley uses **foreshadowing** to alert the audience that there will indeed be both a police investigation and a public scandal before the evening is finished.

Society in 1912 was strictly controlled with a rigid hierarchy of social class. Despite being rich, Mr Birling does not have the social status he craves and desperately wants this knighthood. Priestley condemns this social climbing as it means Birling is more concerned with his status than his responsibilities.

'sharp ring of a front door bell'

- **Stage directions** are used to create dramatic tension. A **stage direction** of a ringing door bell introduces the Inspector.

- The bell cuts across Mr Birling's speech which outlines his views on **'community and all that nonsense'**. The **'sharp'** ring **foreshadows** the impact that the Inspector will have on Mr Birling's life as it demonstrates how the Inspector has the power to interrupt Mr Birling and to challenge him.

- The **stage direction** stops Mr Birling and the sound of it also jolts the audience. It signals a turning point in the play.

'Burnt her inside out, of course'

- Language is used to create dramatic tension. Investigating an incident, Inspector Goole establishes the victim and the nature of her death - that Eva swallowed disinfectant which **'burnt her inside out, of course'**.

- The graphic *vocabulary* of the corrosive liquid destroying Eva's body is shocking to the Birlings and also to the audience. The matter-of-fact *interjection* 'of **course'** only highlights just how appalling the death was; there was no doubt at all about the fatal outcome of her actions.

> By establishing the crime, Priestley follows the formula for a classic whodunnit, a detective story where the audience has to guess who the criminal is. However, the whodunnit is not the definitive genre; 'An Inspector Calls' could fit into the genre of a morality play, a political play or a drama about family life.

'One line of enquiry'

- *Pace* is used to control the tension. The Inspector takes charge of the investigation.

- Inspector Goole controls the *pace* of the story and here he is used by Priestley as a dramatic device to show the crimes of Birlings and the Crofts in a methodical, ruthlessly efficient manner.

'compelled to confess in public his responsibility'

- *Staging* is used to create dramatic tension. Mrs Birling states that the man responsible for Eva/Daisy's pregnancy should be forced to publicly admit his guilt.

- This is a dramatic moment for the audience as it ends Act 2 with a sense of *climax*. We are expecting Eric's imminent arrival as we, like Sheila, can see that it is Eric who will be exposed as the mysterious father.

'Beside, you're not the type- you don't get drunk-'

- Dramatic tension is created through the interaction of the characters. In Act 3, Sybil Birling is still in denial about her son's behaviour.

- Her words reveal her ignorance and her tendency to categorise people- **'you're not the type'**.

- Her *fragmented speech* shows her anxiety as she is forced to confront the truth that the audience has seen since Act 1: that her son drinks too much.

- She is seen as an inadequate mother here as she has been blind to Eric's drinking problems.

'Fire and blood and anguish'

- **Climax** is used to create tension. The Inspector's final speech warns that, if society does not learn lessons of public and private responsibility for the poor and the weak, then it will be taught these lessons in **'fire and blood and anguish'**.

- The **syndetic list** of violent destructive **nouns** signals a clear warning to the Birlings and to the audience.

The Inspector here acts as Priestley's mouthpiece. As a socialist, Priestley firmly believed that society should be organised in a fair and equitable way. The Inspector's warning is very relevant to the 1945/6 audience that, without a fairer society, the horrors of WW1 and and the very recent WW2 will be repeated.

 Grade 9 Exploration: Look at the text in a different way

How does Priestley use structure to create dramatic tension?

Priestley uses the three unities of classical Greek theatre; unity of action, unity of time and unity of place. This means that the story unfolds in real time with no gaps; the effect of this is for the audience to witness the exposure of the series of lies and hidden secrets live on stage, heightening the dramatic tension. The opening of Act 1 forms the **exposition** as the self-satisfied complacency of the Birlings is established with the celebration of the engagement, then the **rising action** occurs as the Inspector enters and begins to uncover the secrets of each of the Birlings and Gerald in turn. There is the **climax** as the Inspector gives his dramatic warning about what will happen if the hypocrisy in society is not addressed, then the **falling action** as the characters deal with the fall-out of the evening's revelations. Yet there is an unexpected final **climax** as the telephone rings at the end of the play with the announcement that a girl has killed herself, which leaves the audience on a note of unexpected tension. We see how the Birlings are doomed to repeat the investigation and there is a warning here to the audience about our own social responsibilities; the tension does not dissipate but stays with us as we leave the theatre.

In Stephen Daldry's famous production, the Birlings' house is on stilts and collapses at the end of the play after the Inspector's investigation. It is a very clear and dramatic demonstration to the audience of just how much of an impact the Inspector had, and how he has completely destroyed the pretences and falsehoods of the Birlings and Crofts.

The ringing door bell stops Mr Birling and jolts the audience. It signals a turning point in the play.

The Inspector exposes the crimes of the Birlings in a ruthlessly methodical manner.

'sharp ring of a front door bell'

'one line of enquiry at a time'

Stage directions create tension.

Pace is used to create tension.

Dramatic Tension

Dramatic tension is created through the interaction between the characters.

How does Priestley use structure to create dramatic tension?

'Besides, you're not the type- you don't get drunk-'

Exposition: the self-satisfied Birlings are introduced
Rising action: the Inspector begins to uncover the secrets

Mrs Birling's *fragmented speech* shows her anxiety as she is forced to confront the truth about her son.

Climax: the Inspector leaves with dark warnings for the future
Falling action: the characters deal with the fall-out
Second climax: telephone rings at the end, shocking the audience

Sample GCSE Exam Question & Answer

Q: How does Priestley create and maintain dramatic tension in 'An Inspector Calls'?

✓ **Make the point that dramatic tension is created through foreshadowing and stage directions**

'An Inspector Calls' is a play that is full of tension, with Priestley using many dramatic devices (techniques) to ensure that the audience is fully engaged. *Foreshadowing* is used to create dramatic tension. Arthur Birling predicts that his knighthood is almost guaranteed, **'so long as we behave ourselves, don't get into the police court or start a scandal- eh? (laughs complacently)**. Priestley uses *foreshadowing* to alert the audience that there will indeed be both a police investigation and a public scandal before the evening is finished. Society in 1912 was strictly controlled with a rigid hierarchy of social class. Despite being rich, Mr Birling does not have the social status he craves and desperately wants this knighthood; Priestley condemns this social climbing that Birling displays through the **'complacent'** chuckle which alienates the audience from his smug arrogance. Dramatic tension is also created through *stage directions* such as the **'sharp ring of a front door bell'** which introduces the Inspector. The bell cuts across Mr Birling's speech which outlines his views on **'community and all that nonsense'**. The **'sharp'** ring *foreshadows* the impact that the Inspector will have on Mr Birling's life as it demonstrates how the Inspector has the power to interrupt Mr Birling and challenge him. The *stage direction* stops Mr Birling and the sound of it also jolts the audience. It signals a turning point in the play.

✓ **Move to the point that dramatic tension is also created through language and pace**

Language is used to create dramatic tension. Investigating an incident, Inspector Goole establishes the victim and the nature of her death - that Eva swallowed disinfectant which **'burnt her inside out, of course'**. The graphic *vocabulary* of the corrosive liquid destroying Eva's body is shocking to the Birlings and also to the audience. The matter-of-fact *interjection* **'of course'** only highlights just how appalling the death was; there was no doubt at all about the fatal outcome of her actions. By establishing the crime, Priestley follows the formula for a classic whodunnit, a detective story where the audience has to guess who the criminal is. However, the whodunnit is not the definitive genre; 'An Inspector Calls' could fit into the genre of a morality play, a political play or a drama about family life. Tension is also maintained through *pace*; the Inspector takes charge of the investigation with **'one line of enquiry at a time'**, controlling the *pace* of the story. Here he is used by Priestley as a dramatic device to show the crimes of Birlings and the Crofts in a methodical, ruthlessly efficient manner.

✓ **Make the point that dramatic tension is constructed through staging and interaction between characters**

Staging is used to create dramatic tension. Mrs Birling states that the man responsible for Eva/Daisy's pregnancy should be **'compelled to confess in public his responsibility'**. This is a dramatic moment for the audience as it ends Act 2 with a sense of climax. We are expecting Eric's imminent arrival as we, like Sheila, can see that it is Eric who will be exposed as the mysterious father. At this point in the play, Sybil Birling is still in denial about her son's behaviour and dramatic tension is created through the interaction of the characters. Her words reveal her ignorance and her tendency to categorise people as she says **'you're not the type'** and her *fragmented speech* shows her anxiety as she is forced to confront the truth that the audience has seen since Act 1: that her son drinks too much.

☑ Explore how structure is used to create dramatic tension

Priestley uses the three unities of classical Greek theatre: unity of action, unity of time and unity of place. This means that the story unfolds in real time with no gaps; the effect of this is for the audience to witness the exposure of the series of lies and hidden secrets live on stage, heightening the dramatic tension. The opening of Act 1 forms the *exposition* as the self-satisfied complacency of the Birlings is established with the celebration of the engagement, then the *rising action* occurs as the Inspector enters and begins to uncover each of the Birlings and Gerald in turn. There is the *climax* as the Inspector gives his dramatic warning about what will happen if the hypocrisy in society is not addressed, then the *falling action* as the characters deal with the fall-out of the evening's revelations. In Stephen Daldry's famous production, the Birlings' house is on stilts and collapses at the end of the play after the Inspector's investigation. It is a very clear and dramatic demonstration to the audience of just how much of an impact the Inspector had, and how he has completely destroyed the pretences and falsehoods of the Birlings and Crofts. Yet there is an unexpected final *climax* as the telephone rings at the end of the play with the announcement that a girl has killed herself, which leaves the audience on a note of unexpected tension. We see how the Birlings are doomed to repeat the investigation and there is a warning here to the audience about our own social responsibilities; the tension does not dissipate but stays with us as we leave the theatre.

Essential Exam Tips

- ☑ **Don't worry about writing a long conclusion. It isn't necessary.**

- ☑ **Aim for four detailed paragraphs; your response will be evaluated on quality not quantity but it's difficult to make your response good if it is brief/lacking in detail.**

9 Generation
Exploration of a theme

The clash between generations is one of the central themes in 'An Inspector Calls'. The younger generation responds to the Inspector's messages in a different way to the older generation, and this causes conflict which adds to the dramatic tension.

'You're squiffy'

- Sheila accuses her brother Eric of being drunk.

- She is confrontational and uses a modern word **'squiffy'** which startles her mother, showing that, as a young woman, she is picking up new ideas. She challenges Eric's drinking, unlike her parents who determinedly ignore it, and in that, Priestley shows us from the beginning that she might be different to the older generation and more susceptible to change.

'Well, it's my duty to keep labour costs down'

- Arthur Birling is forced into answering the Inspector's question about why he refused Eva's request for a wage increase.

- The *interjection* **'well'** suggests that Mr Birling is reluctant to justify himself, yet he does give reasons for his actions, showing that the Inspector has power over him.

- Birling states that he needs to keep **'labour costs down'**. He uses the language of economics which hides the reality of the situation; by keeping wages down, Birling is condemning his workers to lives of poverty and hardship.

- Birling sees his actions as his **'duty'**; while the Inspector's, and Priestley's, duty is to change society, Birling's duty is to make more money.

Capitalism was the economic system which shaped society in 1912. Capitalism meant that rich landowners and factory owners were able to control the labour force, resulting in profit for those in control but often poor living and working conditions for the workers. Priestley was a socialist and wanted to see society change so that there was a fairer distribution of profit and that workers were treated more fairly. Through Birling's defensive, arrogant words, we see Priestley criticise the capitalist system.

'Why shouldn't they try for higher wages? We try for the highest possible prices'

- In Act 1, Eric approves of Eva's attempt to secure a pay rise, telling his father that Eva was justified in trying for higher wages.

- Eric has a different, more equitable (fair) attitude to the workers than his father has. The conflict between them is evident but here Mr Birling shuts his son down effortlessly, showing the power that the older generation wield.

'They just won't try to understand our position or to see the difference between a lot of stuff like this coming out in private and a downright public scandal'

- At the end, when it is realised that the Inspector was a 'fake', Birling sneers at his children for still being troubled by the evening's events.

- He is a character who has learned nothing from the events; he dismisses a girl's suicide and his part in it as **'a lot of stuff'**. This off-hand phrase diminishes the tragedy of Eva's death and shows that he is as arrogant as he was at the beginning of the play. As a member of the older generation, he refuses to learn lessons of social responsibility.

- Birling shows his pretensions to achieve a higher social standing in his desire to avoid a **'public scandal'** that could damage his chances at moving up the social ladder by being given a knighthood. At the end of the play, he is unchanged- as snobbish and unlikeable as at the start.

Edwardian society in 1912 was strictly controlled with a rigid hierarchy of social class. Despite being rich, Mr Birling does not have the social status he craves and is desperate for the knighthood; Priestley condemns this social climbing.

> (shouting) 'And I say the girl's dead and we all helped to kill her– and that's what matters–'

- By the end of Act 3, Eric has changed from the unconfident boy we see in Act 1; here he admits that he killed Eva, blames his family as well and dismisses his father's concerns over public exposure.

- The **stage direction** shows his great passion; earlier in the play he was easily silenced but here he is **'shouting'**, reflecting his desire to be heard and to challenge his parents.

- His **declarative statement** **'we all helped kill her'** clearly states that they are all guilty. The **inclusive pronoun** **'we'** means that no one is allowed to excuse themselves from their actions. Unlike his father, he has learned lessons of social responsibility.

 ## Grade 9 Exploration: Look at the theme in a different way

<u>Are the younger generation a symbol of hope at the end of the play?</u>

Yes: At the end of Act 3, Sheila remembers the Inspector's warning and is worried at how her parents have been unaffected by the evening's events, saying **'fire and blood and anguish. And it frightens me the way you talk'**. Sheila, as part of the younger generation, is a **symbol** of hope for the future; she has changed from the start of the play and is now aware that society also needs to change. The Inspector has the greatest impact on her. She **repeats** the Inspector's warning words, reminding the audience of his dark predictions about what will happen if society does not change. The **syndetic list** of destructive **nouns** reminds the audience of the horror that will be shortly enfolding.

No: We do wonder if there is real hope in the young people. Gerald is also a member of the younger generation yet he has not learned the Inspector's lessons. Gerald's last words of the play are **'What about this ring?'** and this shows his arrogance as he expects everything to return to normal and for Sheila to continue with their marriage plans. His question sounds off-hand and complacent. He has shrugged off the horror of the evening's revelations and is keen to resume his old life, unaffected by the events. Gerald's complacent attitude jars with the audience in his desire for Sheila to take back the ring and we wonder uneasily if the younger generation will be any different to the older generation.

The First World War was, in the eyes of the socialist Priestley, a consequence of the capitalist system that defined European society in the early 20th century. The economic rivalries between Germany, France and Great Britain helped pave the path to war, and so Sheila's anxiety over her parents' refusal to take responsibility for the poor in society is justified. It will be her generation which will be most affected by the two world wars that are coming.

Eric shows a different, more equitable attitude to the workers than his father.

'Why shouldn't they try for higher wages? We try for the highest possible prices.'

Conflict between the generations is evident from the beginning.

Generation

The younger generation learn lessons about responsibility.

(shouting) And I say the girl's dead and we all helped to kill her- and that's what matters-'

His *declarative statement* challenges his parents and shows that he understands that they are all guilty.

At the end, the older Birlings are more concerned with covering up the events than learning from them.

'They just won't try to understand our position or to see the difference between a lot of stuff like this coming out in private and a downright public scandal'

The older generation refuse to learn lessons about responsibility.

Are the younger generation a *symbol* of hope at the end of the play?

Yes: Sheila, as part of the younger generation, is a *symbol* of hope; she has changed from the start of the play and is now aware that society also needs to change.

No: Gerald wants Sheila to take back the ring and revert to normal; we wonder uneasily if the younger generation will be any different to the older generation.

Sample GCSE Exam Question & Answer

Q: How does Priestley present conflict between generations in 'An Inspector Calls'?

☑ Make the point that the conflict between generations is hinted at from the start

The clash between generations is one of the central themes in 'An Inspector Calls'. The younger generation responds to the Inspector's messages in a different way to the older generation, and this causes conflict which adds to the dramatic tension. From the beginning of the play, the audience is aware that there is conflict. Sheila accuses her brother Eric of being drunk, saying **'You're squiffy.'** She is confrontational and uses a modern word **'squiffy'** which startles her mother, showing that, as a young woman, she is picking up new ideas. She challenges Eric's drinking, unlike her parents who determinedly ignore it, and in that, Priestley shows us from the beginning that she might be different to the older generation and more susceptible to change.

☑ Move to the point that generations hold different viewpoints

Mr Birling holds capitalist views, saying **'Well, it's my duty to keep labour costs down'**. Arthur Birling is forced into answering the Inspector's question about why he refused Eva's request for a wage increase. The ***interjection* 'well'** suggests that Mr Birling is reluctant to justify himself, yet he does give reasons for his actions, showing that the Inspector has power over him. Birling states that he needs to keep **'labour costs down'**. This phrase uses the language of economics which disguises the reality of the situation; by keeping wages down, Birling is condemning his workers to lives of poverty and hardship. It is interesting that Birling sees his actions as his **'duty'**; while the Inspector, and Priestley's duty, is a desire to change society, Birling's duty is simply to make more money. Capitalism was the economic system which shaped society in 1912. Capitalism meant that rich landowners and factory owners were able to control the labour force, resulting in profit for those in control but often poor iving and working conditions for the workers. Priestley was a socialist and wanted to see society change so that there was a fairer distribution of profit and that workers were treated more fairly. Through Birling's defensive, arrogant words, we see Priestley criticise the capitalist system. However, the younger Eric has a different attitude, asking, **'Why shouldn't they try for higher wages? We try for the highest possible prices.'** He approves of Eva's attempt to secure a pay rise, telling his father that Eva was justified in trying for higher wages. Eric has a different, more equitable (fair) attitude to the workers than his father has. The conflict between them is evident but here Mr Birling shuts his son down effortlessly, showing the power that the older generation wield.

☑ Make the point that the conflict escalates as the younger generation learn from the Inspector

By the end of the play, the generation divide is very clear. At the end, when it is realised that the Inspector was a 'fake', Birling sneers at his children for still being troubled by the evening's events. **'They just won't try to understand our position or to see the difference between a lot of stuff like this coming out in private and a downright public scandal'**. He is a character who has learned nothing from the events; he dismisses a girl's suicide and his part in it as **'a lot of stuff'**. This off-hand phrase diminishes the tragedy of Eva's death and shows that he is as arrogant as he was at the beginning of the play. Birling shows his pretensions to achieve a higher social standing in his desire to avoid a **'public scandal'** that could damage his chances at moving up the social ladder by being given a knighthood. At the end of the play, he is unchanged- as snobbish and unlikeable as at the start. Pre world war society in 1912 was strictly controlled with a rigid hierarchy of social class. Despite being rich, Mr Birling does not have the social status he craves and is desperate for this knighthood; Priestley condemns this social climbing. Yet Eric is a marked contrast to his father's attitude; he does not care about social status and is fully aware of his responsibilities, **(shouting) 'And I say the girl's dead and we all helped to kill her- and that's what matters-'**. By the end of Act 3, Eric has changed from the unconfident boy we see in Act 1; here he admits that he killed Eva, blames his family as well and dismisses his father's concerns over public exposure. The *stage direction* shows his great passion; earlier in the play he was easily silenced but here he is **'shouting'**, reflecting his desire to be heard and to challenge his family. His *declarative statement* **'we all helped kill her'** clearly states that they are all guilty. The *inclusive pronoun* **'we'** means that no one is allowed to excuse themselves from their actions. The difference between the generations is shown through these wildly different responses to the Inspector and his messages.

☑ Explore whether the younger generation is a symbol of hope at the end of the play

At the end of Act 3, Sheila remembers the Inspector's warning and is worried at how her parents have been unaffected by the evening's events: **'Fire and blood and anguish. And it frightens me the way you talk'**. Sheila, as part of the younger generation, is a *symbol* of hope for the future; she has changed from the start of the play and is now aware that society also needs to change. The Inspector has the greatest impact on her. She *repeats* the Inspector's warning words, reminding the audience of his dark predictions about what will happen if society does not change. The *syndetic list* of destructive *nouns* reminds the audience of the horror that will be shortly enfolding. The First World War was, in the eyes of the socialist Priestley, a consequence of the capitalist system that defined European society in the early 20th century. The economic rivalries between Germany, France and Great Britain helped pave the path to war, and so Sheila's anxiety over her parents' refusal to take responsibility for the poor in society is justified. It will be her generation which will be most affected by the two world wars that are coming. Yet we do wonder if there is real hope for change in the young people. Gerald is also a member of the younger generation yet he has not learned the Inspector's lessons. Gerald's last words of the play are **'What about this ring?'**; this shows his arrogance as he expects everything to return to normal and for Sheila to continue with their marriage plans. His question sounds off-hand and complacent. He has shrugged off the horror of the evening's revelations and is keen to resume his old life, unaffected by the events. Gerald's complacent attitude jars with the audience in his desire for Sheila to take back the ring and we wonder uneasily if the younger generation will be any different to the older generation.

Essential Exam Tips

- ☑ Learn quotations off by heart. Write them out on sticky labels and put them by the kettle or on the bathroom mirror-places where you go to all of the time.

- ☑ Use the word Priestley! It sounds silly but you need to write about what Priestley is doing. So use phrases such as 'Priestley presents/Priestley uses'.

The Birlings and Gerald Croft begin the play with a facade of perfect happiness and harmony yet the Inspector's investigation shows us how their lives are built on fragile webs of lies and hypocrisy.

'When you never came near me, and I wondered what had happened to you'

- Despite the happiness of the engagement, Sheila refers to the summer when Gerald had been inexplicably distant.

- Even at the opening of the play, we see hints of unrevealed deceit and hypocrisy in the relationships. Sheila does not fully trust her fiance. There is an underlying tension that audiences pick up on, **foreshadowing** the future turmoil that the exposure of the lies will bring.

'brighter and harder'

- When the Inspector first comes on stage, the lighting changes to become **'brighter and harder'**.

- This **stage direction** shows how the Inspector destroys the cosy, intimate atmosphere; the lighting reflects his power as, when he enters, it becomes **'brighter and harder'**, turning a spotlight on the lies and hypocrisy at the heart of the Birling household. His control is clear as he **'takes charge' 'cutting in'** and forcing all the Birlings, including the impregnable Mrs Birling, to admit their part in Eva's death.

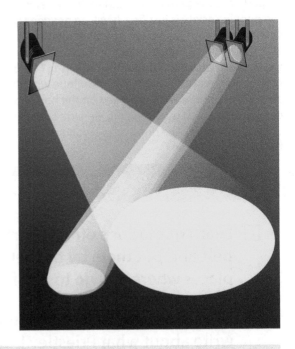

In Stephen Daldry's famous production, the Birlings' house is on stilts and collapses at the end of the play after the Inspector's investigation. It is a very clear and dramatic demonstration to the audience of just how much of an impact the Inspector had, and how he has completely destroyed the pretences and falsehoods of the Birlings and Crofts.

'One line of enquiry at a time'

- The Inspector takes charge of the investigation.

- Inspector Goole controls the *pace* of the story. Priestley uses him as a dramatic device to expose the lies of the Birlings and the Crofts in a methodical, ruthlessly efficient manner.

'Well, it's my duty to keep labour costs down'

- Arthur Birling is forced into answering the Inspector's question about why he refused Eva's request for a wage increase.

- The *interjection* **'well'** suggests that Mr Birling is reluctant to justify himself, yet he does give reasons for his actions. This shows that the Inspector has power over him as he is forced to admit what he did and is exposed as a hypocrite.

- Birling states that he needs to keep **'labour costs down'**. This phrase uses the language of economics which disguises the reality of the situation; by keeping wages down, Birling is condemning his workers to lives of poverty and hardship. His language choices show his hypocrisy as he hides behind economics to justify poverty.

Priestley was a socialist and wanted to see society change so that there was a fairer distribution of profit and that workers were treated more fairly. Through Birling's defensive, arrogant words, we see Priestley criticise the capitalist system and expose it as a hypocritical system which promises wealth but delivers poverty.

'They just won't try to understand our position or to see the difference between a lot of stuff like this coming out in private and a downright public scandal'

- At the end, when it is realised that the Inspector was a 'fake', Birling sneers at his children for still being troubled by the evening's events.

- He is a character who has learned nothing from the events; he dismisses a girl's suicide and his part in it as **'a lot of stuff'**. This off-hand phrase diminishes the tragedy of Eva's death and shows that he is as arrogant as he was at the beginning of the play. He is still more interested in public facades than in doing the right thing; his hypocrisy is unchanged.

- Birling shows his pretensions to achieve a higher social standing in his desire to avoid a **'public scandal'** that could damage his chances at moving up the social ladder by being given a knighthood. At the end of the play, he is unchanged- and as snobbish and unlikeable as at the start.

> **(shouting) 'And I say the girl's dead and we all helped to kill her- and that's what matters-'**

- Eric has changed from the unconfident boy we see in Act 1; here he admits that he killed Eva, blames his family as well and dismisses his father's concerns over public exposure.

- The *stage direction* shows his great passion for them all to acknowledge the truth; earlier in the play he was easily silenced but here he is **'shouting'**, reflecting his desire to be heard and to challenge his family to honestly accept their share of responsibility.

- His *declarative statement* **'we all helped kill her'** clearly states that they are guilty. The inclusive *pronoun* **'we'** means that no one is allowed to excuse themselves from their actions.

- Eric, as part of the younger generation, is a *symbol* of hope for the future; he has changed from the beginning of the play and is now aware that society also needs to change and be more fair and honest in its dealings with all people.

 ## Grade 9 Exploration: Look at the theme in a different way

How is structure used to expose the lies and hypocrisy?

Priestley uses the three unities of classical Greek theatre; unity of action, unity of time and unity of place. This means that the story unfolds in real time with no gaps; the effect of this is for the audience to witness the exposure of the series of lies and hidden secrets live on stage, heightening the dramatic tension. The opening of Act 1 forms the *exposition* as the self-satisfied complacency of the Birlings is established with the celebration of the engagement, then the *rising action* occurs as the Inspector enters and begins to uncover each of the secrets of the Birlings and Gerald in turn. There is the *climax* as the Inspector gives his dramatic warning about what will happen if the hypocrisy in society is not addressed, then the *falling action* as the characters deal with the fall-out of the evening's revelations. Yet there is an unexpected final *climax* as the telephone rings at the end of the play with the announcement that a girl has killed herself and an inspector is on his way, which leaves the audience on a note of unexpected tension, and the Birlings and Gerald with absolutely nowhere else to hide.

There is an underlying tension that the audience picks up on, *foreshadowing* the future turmoil that the exposure of the lies will bring.

↑

'When you never came near me, and I wondered what had happened to you'

↑

Relationships are based on deceit and lies.

This *stage direction* shows how the Inspector destroys the cosy atmosphere as he begins to expose the lies and hypocrisy at the heart of the Birling household.

↑

'brighter and harder'

↑

The Inspector uncovers the lies and hypocrisy.

Lies & Hypocrisy

The younger generation understands that society needs to be more open and honest.

↓

(shouting) 'And I say the girl's dead and we all helped to kill her- and that's what matters-'

↓

The *stage direction* shows Eric's great passion for them all to acknowledge the truth.

How is structure used to expose the lies and hypocrisy?

↓

Exposition: the self-satisfied Birlings are introduced
Rising action: the Inspector begins to uncover the secrets

↓

Climax: the Inspector leaves with dark warnings for the future
Falling action: the characters deal with the fall-out
Second climax: telephone rings at the end. There is nowhere to hide.

Sample GCSE Exam Question & Answer

Q: How does Priestley show that lies and hypocrisy are at the heart of the Birlings' household?

☑ Make the point that lies and hypocrisy lie at the heart of the Birlings' household

The Birlings and Gerald Croft begin the play with a facade of perfect happiness and harmony yet the Inspector's investigation shows us how their lives are built on fragile webs of lies and hypocrisy. Even at the opening of the play, we see hints of unrevealed deceit and hypocrisy in the relationships. Despite the happiness of the engagement, Sheila refers to the summer when Gerald had been inexplicably distant: **'When you never came near me, and I wondered what had happened to you'**. Sheila does not fully trust her fiance. There is an underlying tension that the audience picks up on, *foreshadowing* the future turmoil that the exposure of the lies will bring.

☑ Move to the point that the Inspector's role is to expose the lies and deceit

When the Inspector first comes on stage, the lighting changes to become **'brighter and harder'**. This *stage direction* shows how the Inspector destroys the cosy, intimate atmosphere as he begins to turn the spotlight on the lies and hypocrisy at the heart of the Birling household. His control is clear as he **'takes charge' 'cutting in'** and forcing all the Birlings, including the impregnable Mrs Birling, to admit their part in Eva's death. In Stephen Daldry's famous production, the Birlings' house is on stilts and collapses at the end of the play after the Inspector's investigation. It is a very clear and dramatic demonstration to the audience of just how much of an impact the Inspector had, and how he has completely destroyed the pretences and falsehoods of the Birlings and Crofts. The Inspector does this by taking charge of the investigation with **'one line of enquiry at a time'** and so controlling the *pace* of the story; here, the Inpsector is a dramatic device used by Priestley to show the lies of the Birlings and the Crofts in a methodical, ruthlessly efficient manner.

☑ Make the point that the Birlings are divided in whether they accept the truth of their actions

The older generation refuse to accept the truth: that their actions do have an impact on wider society. At the end, when it is realised that the Inspector was a 'fake', Birling sneers at his children for still being troubled by the evening's events. He is a character who has learned nothing from the events; he dismisses a girl's suicide and his part in it as **'a lot of stuff'**. This off-hand phrase diminishes the tragedy of Eva's death and shows that the Inspector's warnings have not touched Birling. He is still more interested in public facades than in doing the right thing; his hypocrisy is unchanged. Birling shows his pretensions to achieve a higher social standing in his desire to avoid a **'public scandal'** that could damage his chances at moving up the social ladder by being given a knighthood. At the end of the play, he is unchanged- and as snobbish and unlikeable as at the start. Society in 1912 was strictly controlled with a rigid hierarchy of social class. Despite being rich, Mr Birling does not have the social status he craves and is desperate for this knighthood. Priestley condemns this social climbing and the hypocrisy and artifice it leads to. It is the younger generation who learn lessons from the exposure of the lies and hypocrisy. In Act 3, Eric states, **(shouting) 'And I say the girl's dead and we all helped to kill her- and that's what matters'**. Eric has changed from the unconfident boy we see in Act 1; here he admits that he killed Eva, blames his family as well and dismisses his father's concerns over public exposure. The *stage direction* shows his great passion for them all to acknowledge the truth; earlier in the play he was easily silenced but here he is **'shouting'**, reflecting his desire to be heard and to challenge his family to honestly accept their share of responsibility. His *declarative statement* 'we all

helped kill her' clearly states that they are guilty. The *inclusive pronoun* **'we'** means that no one is allowed to excuse themselves from their actions. Eric, as part of the younger generation, is a *symbol* of hope for the future; he has changed from the beginning of the play and is now aware that society also needs to change and be more fair and honest in its dealings with all people.

☑ Explore how Priestley uses structure to expose the lies and hypocrisy

Priestley uses the three unities of classical Greek theatre; unity of action, unity of time and unity of place. This means that the story unfolds in real time with no gaps; the effect of this is for the audience to witness the exposure of the series of lies and hidden secrets live on stage, heightening the dramatic tension. The opening of Act 1 forms the *exposition* as the self-satisfied complacency of the Birlings is established with the celebration of the engagement, then the *rising action* occurs as the Inspector enters and begins to uncover each of the Birlings and Gerald in turn. There is the *climax* as the Inspector gives his dramatic warning about what will happen if the hypocrisy in society is not addressed, then the *falling action* as the characters deal with the fall-out of the evening's revelations. Yet there is an unexpected final *climax* as the telephone rings at the end of the play with the announcement that a girl has killed herself, which leaves the audience on a note of unexpected tension. By the end of the play, with another investigation pending, we can see that the Birlings and Gerald have no place left to hide.

Essential Exam Tips

- ☑ **Re-read the play about a fortnight before the exam from start to finish. It should only take a couple of hours to do this.**

- ☑ **Watch a film or TV version of the play at least once.**

11 Social Class
Exploration of a theme

The theme of social class is at the heart of the play. The plot of the play revolves around how Eva Smith/Daisy Renton, a working class girl, is exploited and abused by members of the wealthy upper classes.

'good solid furniture' 'living in lodgings'

- The opening *stage directions* establish the wealth of the Birling family.

- There is a sense of stability and prosperity in the staging and this is enhanced by the props such as **'champagne glasses'**.

- Later, the Inspector describes how Eva is alone and poor: **'living in lodgings'**.

- The word **'lodgings'** suggests temporary, bleak accommodation which *contrasts* with the **'good solid furniture'** and reminds the audience about the difference in the lifestyles between the upper classes and the lower classes.

'Well, it's my duty to keep labour costs down'

- Arthur Birling is forced into answering the Inspector's question about why he refused Eva's request for a wage increase.

- Birling states that he needs to keep **'labour costs down'**. This phrase uses the language of economics which disguises the reality of the situation; by keeping wages down, the wealthy Mr Birling is condemning his workers to lives of poverty and hardship.

Priestley was a socialist and wanted to see society change so that there was a fairer distribution of profit and that workers were treated more fairly. Through Birling's defensive, arrogant words, we see Priestley criticise the capitalist system which helped prop up the upper classes at the expense of the lower classes.

'girls of that class'

- Mrs Birling dismisses Eva Smith as **'girls of that class'**. She sees Eva as just one of many working girls. By grouping the girls together, she shows a lack of humanity; she sees them as a type, not as individuals. There is a sense of snobbery in the *determiner* **'that'** which distances herself from them.

Society in 1912 was strictly controlled with a rigid hierarchy of social class. Mrs Birling firmly believes in this social system and this belief is evident in her choice of language.

'As if a girl of that sort would ever refuse money!'

- Mrs Birling laughs at the idea of Eva turning down the stolen money from Eric, yet this is exactly what Eva did.

- Eva is shown as a girl of strong morals, refusing to accept the money which came from crime. Despite being poor and desperate, she is seen as morally superior to the Birlings and Crofts, with an integrity (honesty) that they lack.

Priestley challenges the rigid class system which assumed that those born into a high class were 'better' than the working class.

'They just won't try to understand our position or to see the difference between a lot of stuff like this coming out in private and a downright public scandal'

- At the end, when it is realised that the Inspector was a 'fake', Birling sneers at his children for still being troubled by the evening's events.

- He is a character who has learned nothing from the events; he dismisses a girl's suicide and his part in it as **'a lot of stuff'**. This off-hand phrase diminishes the tragedy of Eva's death and shows that he is as arrogant as he was at the beginning of the play. He is still more interested in public facades than in doing the right thing; his hypocrisy is unchanged.

- Birling shows his pretensions to achieve a higher social standing in his desire to avoid a **'public scandal'** that could damage his chances at moving up the social ladder by being given a knighthood. At the end of the play, he is unchanged- as snobbish and unlikeable as at the start.

Despite being rich, Mr Birling does not have the social status he craves and is desperate for the knighthood; Priestley condemns this social climbing.

'Fire and blood and anguish. And it frightens me the way you talk'

- At the end of Act 3, Sheila remembers the Inspector's warning and is worried at how her parents have been unaffected by the evening's events.

- Sheila's generation is the one that will be affected by the refusal of her parents to take responsibility for the poor in society or to change their attitudes to the lower classes.

- She **repeats** the Inspector's warning words, reminding the audience of his dark predictions of what will happen if society does not change. The **syndetic list** of destructive **nouns** reminds the audience of the horror that will be shortly unfolding.

The First World War was, in the eyes of the socialist Priestley, a consequence of the capitalist system that defined European society in the early 20th century. The economic rivalries between Germany, France and Great Britain helped pave the path to war, and so Sheila's anxiety over her parents' refusal to take responsibility for the poor in society is justified. It will be her generation which will be most affected by the two world wars that are coming.

 ## Grade 9 Exploration: Look at the theme in a different way

Is 'An Inspector Calls' primarily a political play about class?

Yes: Priestley was a committed socialist and wrote the play at the end of the Second World War, when the Labour Party was coming to power with promises of free health service and a fairer, more equitable society. The play consistently reflects Priestley's beliefs as he tries to show the audience that there are still **'millions and millions and millions of Eva Smiths'** to be considered and to take responsibility for.

No: The genre of the play is ambiguous. Priestley follows the formula for a classic whodunnit, a detective story where the audience has to guess who the criminal is. However, the whodunnit is not the definitive genre and 'An Inspector Calls' could fit into the category of a morality play. These were plays performed in the Middle Ages which taught audiences how to behave through repentance of the deadly sins and certainly the Birlings and Gerald between them represent all seven deadly sins. Yet perhaps the play is primarily a portrayal of family relationships; after all, the audience is fully engaged as we watch the relationships between the characters change throughout the story.

The *stage directions* establish the Birlings as living in wealth and comfort. This *contrasts* with Eva who lives in temporary accommodation.

Mr Birling holds power. He puts profit over the wages and living conditions of his workers.

'good solid furniture'
'living in lodgings'

'Well, it's my duty to keep labour costs down'

Priestley exposes the difference in lifestyles between the upper and lower classes.

Priestley shows the audience how the working classes are exploited.

Social Class

The younger generation understand that the way society is organised is flawed and needs to change.

Is 'An Inspector Calls' primarily a political play about class?

'Fire and blood and anguish. And it frightens me the way you talk'

Yes: The play reflects Priestley's beliefs that the rich in society have a social responsibility to protect the poor.

Sheila sees that attitudes to the working classes need to change otherwise there wil be dreadful consequences.

No: The play could be a whodunnit, a modern morality play or a play about family relationships.

Sample GCSE Exam Question & Answer

Q: Explore how far 'An Inspector Calls' is a political play about social class.

☑ Start with the point that the division of social class is established from the opening of the play

The theme of social class is at the heart of the play. The plot of the play revolves around how Eva Smith/Daisy Renton, a working class girl, is exploited and abused by members of the wealthy upper classes. This is shown from the opening *stage directions* which establish the wealth of the Birling family: **'good solid furniture'**. There is a sense of stability and prosperity in the staging and this is enhanced by the props such as **'champagne glasses'**. Later, the Inspector describes how Eva is alone and poor: **'living in lodgings'**. The word **'lodgings'** suggests temporary, bleak accommodation which *contrasts* with the **'good solid furniture'** and reminds the audience about the difference in the lifestyles between the upper classes and the lower classes.

☑ Move to the point that Priestley uses the characters to show how the lower classes are exploited and abused

Mr Birling sees it as his duty to exploit the working classes, being forced into answering the Inspector's question about why he refused Eva's request for a wage increase saying **'Well, it's my duty to keep labour costs down'**. This phrase uses the language of economics which disguises the reality of the situation; by keeping wages down, the wealthy Mr Birling is condemning his workers to lives of poverty and hardship. It is interesting that Birling sees his actions as his **'duty'**; while the Inspector's, and Priestley's, duty is a desire to change society, Birling's duty is simply to make more money. Priestley was a socialist and wanted to see society change so that there was a fairer distribution of profit and that workers were treated more fairly. Through Birling's defensive, arrogant words, we see Priestley criticise the capitalist system which helped prop up the upper classes at the expense of the lower classes. Similarly, Priestley uses Mrs Birling to show how she despises the working classes. Mrs Birling dismisses Eva Smith as **'girls of that class'**. She sees Eva as just one of many working girls. By grouping the girls together, she shows a lack of humanity; she sees them as a type, not as individuals. There is a sense of snobbery in the *determiner* **'that'** which distances herself from them. Society in 1912 was strictly controlled with a rigid hierarchy of social class; Mrs Birling firmly believes in this social system and this belief is evident in her choice of language.

☑ Move to the point that Priestley is warning the audience that attitudes to class need to change

At the end of Act 3, Sheila remembers the Inspector's warning and is worried at how her parents have been unaffected by the evening's events, saying **'Fire and blood and anguish. And it frightens me the way you talk'**. Sheila's generation is the one that will be affected by the refusal of her parents to take responsibility for the poor in society or to change their attitudes to the lower classes. She *repeats* the Inspector's warning words, reminding the audience of his dark predictions of what will happen if society does not change. The *syndetic list* of destructive *nouns* reminds the audience of the horror that will be shortly unfolding. The First World War was, in the eyes of the socialist Priestley, a consequence of the capitalist system that defined European society in the early 20th century. The economic rivalries between Germany, France and Great Britain helped pave the path to war, and so Sheila's anxiety over her parents' refusal to take responsibility for the poor in society is justified. It will be her generation which will be most affected by the two world wars that are coming.

☑ Explore whether AIC is primarily a political play

There can be little doubt that the play is politically motivated. Priestley was a committed socialist and wrote the play at the end of the Second World War, when the Labour Party was coming to power with promises of free health service and a fairer, more equitable society. The play consistently reflects Priestley's beliefs as he tried to show the audience that there are still '**millions and millions and millions of Eva Smiths'** to be considered and to take responsibility for. Yet this is, perhaps, only one aspect to the play and arguably the genre of the play is ambiguous. Priestley follows the formula for a classic whodunnit, a detective story where the audience has to guess who the criminal is. However, the whodunnit is not the definitive genre and 'An Inspector Calls' could fit into the category of a morality play. These were plays performed in the Middle Ages which taught audiences how to behave through repentance of the deadly sins, and certainly the Birlings and Gerald between them represent all seven deadly sins. Yet perhaps the play is primarily a portrayal of family relationships; after all, the audience is fully engaged as we watch the relationships between the characters change throughout the story.

Essential Exam Tips

☑ Try not to stress about your exams; mindfulness techniques can really help you relax and focus.

☑ Start revising for the exams early. Revising in 10 minutes bursts from the end of Year 10 can make a huge difference and reduces the last minute panic before your exams.

One of the central themes to the play is responsibility: the need for individuals and businesses to behave in a way that benefits society as a whole.

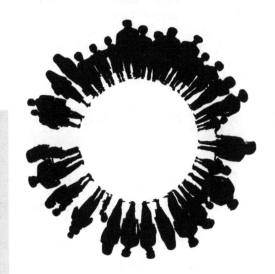

'community and all that nonsense'

- Mr Birling states that we only have a responsibility to ourselves and to our families; he dismisses the idea of community and social responsibility as **'nonsense'**.

- There is an arrogance and an ignorance in his dismissive, contemptuous *tone*.

Priestley was a socialist and believed that a fairer way of organising society and industry would result in a better world. We already distrust Mr Birling's judgement because of his comments on the Titanic being unsinkable, and here Priestley shows how misguided and selfish Mr Birling is.

'sharp ring of a front door bell'

- A *stage direction* of a ringing door bell introduces the Inspector.

- The bell cuts across Mr Birling's speech which outlines his views on **'community and all that nonsense'**. The **'sharp ring'** *foreshadows* the impact that the Inspector will have on Mr Birling's life as it demonstrates how the Inspector has the power to interrupt Mr Birling and challenge him. The Inspector is a dramatic device to teach the Birlings about responsibility.

- The *stage direction* stops Mr Birling and the sound also jolts the audience. It signals a turning point in the play.

'Well, it's my duty to keep labour costs down'

- Birling states that he needs to keep **'labour costs down'**.

- This phrase uses the language of economics which disguises the reality of the situation; by keeping wages down, Birling is condemning his workers to lives of poverty and hardship. He shows a lack of responsibility of an employer to his employees.

- It is interesting that Birling sees his actions as his **'duty'**; while the Inspector's, and Priestley's, duty is a desire to change society, Birling's duty is simply to make more money. Priestley wanted a fairer distribution of profit so that workers were treated more fairly. Through Birling's defensive, arrogant words, we see Priestley criticise capitalism and the way it appears to give employers the opportunity to avoid taking any social responsibility.

'fire and blood and anguish'

- The Inspector's final speech warns that, if society does not learn lessons of public and private responsibility for the poor and the weak, then it will be taught these lessons in **'fire and blood and anguish'**.

- The *syndetic list* of violent destructive *nouns* signals a clear warning to the Birlings and to the audience.

The Inspector here acts as Priestley's mouthpiece. As a socialist, Priestley firmly believed that society should be organised in a fair and equitable way. The Inspector's warning is very relevant to the 1945/6 audience that, without a fairer society, the horrors of World War 1 and World War 2 will be repeated.

> **(shouting)** 'And I say the girl's dead and we all helped to kill her- and that's what matters-'

- By the end of Act 3, Eric has changed from the unconfident boy we see in Act 1; here he admits that he killed Eva, blames his family as well and dismisses his father's concerns over public exposure.

- The *stage direction* shows his great passion; earlier in the play he was easily silenced but here he is **'shouting'**, reflecting his desire to be heard and to challenge his parents.

- His *declarative statement* **'we all helped to kill her'** clearly states that they are all guilty. The *inclusive pronoun* **'we'** means that no one is allowed to excuse themselves from their actions. Unlike his father, he has learned lessons of social responsibility.

Grade 9 Exploration: Look at the theme in a different way

How successful is the play in showing the need for social responsibility?

Very: The Inspector's final words emphatically and clearly tell the audience that **'We don't live alone. We are members of one body. We are responsible for one another'**. These simple, *declarative statements* are immensely hard-hitting as part of the *climax* of the play and therefore leave the audience with a powerful message about the necessity of taking social responsibility.

Limited: At the end, when it is realised that the Inspector was a 'fake', Birling sneers at his children for still being troubled by the evening's events, saying **'They just won't try to understand our position or to see the difference between a lot of stuff like this coming out in private and a downright public scandal'**. He is a character who has learned nothing from the events; he dismisses a girl's suicide and his part in it as **'a lot of stuff'**. This off-hand phrase diminishes the tragedy of Eva's death and shows that he is as arrogant as he was at the beginning of the play. His attitude reminds us that it is part of the human condition to be selfish, and our own societies over 70 years later still lack full and comprehensive social responsibility.

There is an arrogance and contempt in Mr Birling's *tone* yet the audience already distrusts him.

The 'sharp ring' demonstrates how the Inspector has the power to interrupt Mr Birling and challenge him.

'community and all that nonsense'

'sharp ring of a front door bell'

The characters start without any sense of social responsibility.

The Inspector teaches the characters social responsibility.

Social Responsibility

The younger generation learn lessons of social responsibility.

How successful is the play in showing the need for social responsibility?

(shouting) 'And I say the girl's dead and we all helped to kill her- and that's what matters-'

Very: The Inspector's final words emphatically and clearly tell the audience that 'We don't live alone.'

The *inclusive pronoun* 'we' shows that Eric understands that they all have a social responsibility towards the poor.

No: Characters such as Arthur Birling learn nothing; it is part of the human condition to be selfish.

Sample GCSE Exam Question & Answer

Q: How does Priestley explore ideas about social responsibility in the play?

☑ **Make the point that the Birlings start the play oblivious to ideas of social responsibility**

The Birlings start the play oblivious to ideas of social responsibility. Mr Birling states that we only have a responsibility to ourselves and to our families; he rejects the idea of social responsibility as **'community and all that nonsense'**. There is an arrogance and an ignorance in his dismissive, contemptuous tone. Priestley was a socialist and believed that a fairer way of organising society and industry would result in a better world. We already distrust Mr Birling's judgement because of his comments on the Titanic being unsinkable, and here Priestley shows how misguided and selfish Mr Birling is. It is the Inspector who begins to teach the Birlings ideas about social responsibility; a *stage direction* of a **'sharp ring of a front door bell'** introduces the Inspector. The bell cuts across Mr Birling's speech which outlines his views on **'community and all that nonsense'**. The **'sharp ring'** *foreshadows* the impact that the Inspector will have on Mr Birling's life as it demonstrates how the Inspector has the power to interrupt Mr Birling and challenge him. The Inspector is a dramatic device to teach the Birlings about responsibility and the *stage direction* stops Mr Birling and the sound also jolts the audience. It signals a turning point in the play.

☑ **Develop this point that the Inspector's role is to show the Birlings the importance of taking responsibility**

When the Inspector first comes on stage, the lighting changes to become **'brighter and harder'**. This *stage direction* shows how the Inspector destroys the cosy, intimate atmosphere as he begins to unpick the lies and hypocrisy at the heart of the Birling household. The change in lighting reflects the power of the Inspector to force the Birlings to change their selfish outlook and to accept their share of social responsibility. In Stephen Daldry's famous production, the Birlings' house in on stilts and collapses at the end of the play after the Inspector's investigation. It is a very clear and dramatic demonstration to the audience of just how much of an impact the Inspector had, and how he has completely destroyed the bubble of selfishness of the Birlings and Crofts. This power is also seen when Arthur Birling is forced into answering the Inspector's question about why he refused Eva's request for a wage increase. He says **'Well, it's my duty to keep labour costs down'** and the *interjection* **'well'** suggests that Mr Birling is reluctant to justify himself, yet he does give reasons for his actions, showing that the Inspector has power over him. Birling states that he needs to keep **'labour costs down'**. This phrase uses the language of economics which disguises the reality of the situation; by keeping wages down, Birling is condemning his workers to lives of poverty and hardship. He shows a lack of responsibility of an employer to his employees. It is interesting that Birling sees his actions as his **'duty'**; while the Inspector's, and Priestley's, duty is a desire to change society, Birling's duty is simply to make more money. Priestley wanted a fairer distribution of profit so that workers were treated more fairly. Through Birling's defensive, arrogant words, we see Priestley criticise capitalism and the way it appears to give employers the opportunity to avoid taking any social responsibility.

☑ **Move to the point that the Birlings begin to change their attitude to social responsibility**

By the end of Act 3, Eric has changed from the unconfident boy we see in Act 1 as he is **(shouting) And I say the girl's dead and we all helped to kill her- and that's what matters-'**. He admits that he killed Eva, blames his family as well and dismisses his father's concerns over public exposure. The *stage direction* shows his great passion; earlier in the play he was easily silenced but here he is **'shouting'**, reflecting his desire to be heard and to challenge his family to honestly accept their share of responsibility. His *declarative statement* **'we all helped to kill her'** clearly states that they are guilty. The *inclusive pronoun* **'we'** means that no one is allowed to excuse themselves from their actions; they must all accept a share in the responsibility for Eva's death.

☑ Explore how successful the play is in showing the need for social responsibility

Yet we do wonder how much of an impact the Inspector has. At the end, when it is realised that the Inspector was a 'fake', Birling sneers at his children for still being troubled by the evening's events, saying **'They just won't try to understand our position or to see the difference between a lot of stuff like this coming out in private and a downright public scandal'**. He is a character who has learned nothing from the events; he dismisses a girl's suicide and his part in it as **'a lot of stuff'**. This off-hand phrase diminishes the tragedy of Eva's death and shows that he is still as arrogant as he was at the beginning of the play. His attitude reminds us that it is part of the human condition to be selfish, and our own societies over 70 years later still lack full and comprehensive social responsibility. We can only hope that others, such as Eric and Sheila, do not forget the lessons they have learned from the Inspector whose final words emphatically and clearly tells the audience that **'We don't live alone. We are members of one body. We are responsible for one another'**. These simple, *declarative statements* are immensely hard-hitting as part of the *climax* of the play and therefore leave the audience with a powerful message of the necessity of social responsibility.

Essential Exam Tips

☑ Underline the focus of the question so you don't stray from answering the question. E.g. in the question above, the focus is social responsibility.

☑ Try to add comments about stage directions when you write your response.

13 Love & Relationships
Exploration of a theme

The opening of the play is, on the surface, a celebration of love in the engagement of Sheila and Gerald, and the audience initially sees a family which seems close. Yet the Inspector methodically and thoroughly reveals the weaknesses in these relationships.

'you'll have to get used to that, just as I had'

- Mrs Birling tells Sheila that Sheila will have to allow Gerald to work long hours away from her: **'you'll have to get used to that, just as I had'**.

- Mr and Mrs Birling's marriage is unequal. Mrs Birling has had to put up with her husband being absent at the factory for extended periods of time. There is acceptance in her *tone* at this situation but it could be that their marriage has been damaged by Mr Birling's attention to his business.

  - **In 1912 British society, upper class women's lives were restricted to the domestic sphere and women were expected to defer to the needs and wishes of their husbands.**

'Your engagement to Sheila means a tremendous lot to me'

- Mr Birling tells Gerald how pleased he is about the engagement, and continues his speech about the joining of the two families, finishing with talking about lower costs and prices.

- He sees the relationship, in part, as a business transaction. The marriage will ally the two families closely together which will be good for business.

- It is probable that his own marriage was based on financial transactions. He is from a lower social class than Mrs Birling.

'When you never came near me, and I wondered what had happened to you'

- Despite the happiness of the engagement, Sheila refers to the summer when Gerald had been inexplicably distant.

- Even at the opening of the play, we see hints of underlying deceit and hypocrisy in the relationships. Sheila does not fully trust her fiance. This *foreshadows* the later fracturing of their relationship.

'Oh- it's wonderful! Look- Mummy- isn't it a beauty?'

- Sheila is excited about her engagement ring, showing it to her mother. She is clearly delighted with it; her fragmented speech, indicated through the *dashes*, shows her great excitement.

- She warms to Gerald, forgetting about the tension caused by his evasion about his distance in the summer. She comes across as shallow as she is so easily won over by a sparkling expensive ring and we wonder if this relationship is based on material considerations rather than true love.

There were limited options for employment and education for women in 1912 and women were expected to marry and bring up children. Sheila might be shallow in her excitement over the ring but she is restricted by the time period in which she lives and, by the standards of her society, she has achieved highly by securing a wealthy husband.

(sharp sarcasm) 'You were the wonderful Fairy Prince'

- Sheila is bitter in her statement that Gerald was Daisy's fairy-tale prince as he tells the story of how he rescued her from one unpleasant situation but then used her as his mistress.
- The *stage direction* 'sharp sarcasm' shows how disillusioned Sheila has become with her well-mannered fiance. The *tone* alerts the audience that Gerald has abused his position and that there was nothing **'wonderful'** about his behaviour.

As a poor girl in 1912, Daisy/Eva would have been in a vulnerable position and it would have been easy for the wealthy Gerald to take advantage of this.

'As I'm rather more- upset... and- well, I'd like to be alone'

- Gerald is emotionally affected by the realisation that his ex-lover has committed suicide.

- The *fragmented speech* indicated by the *ellipsis* and *dashes* show his agitation and grief.

> **'I was in that state when a chap easily turns nasty'**
> **'used her... as if she was an animal, a thing, not a person'**

- Eric admits that he forced himself into Eva/Daisy's house and also forced her to have sex, as he was drunk and on the verge of violence.

- The relationship with Daisy was one based on sex, violence and abuse of power.

- Yet he uses the *noun* **'chap'** to describe himself; it has the effect of making him sound jolly and rather harmless. Later, the Inspector tells him clearly that his behaviour was disgusting, that Eric treated Daisy **'as if she was an animal, a thing, not a person'**. The *list* shows how Eric abused his position as a rich man of great privilege by diminishing a lonely, poor girl and seeing her as sub-human- an **'animal'** and even an object- **'a thing'**.

> Priestley drew upon conventions of morality plays; these were plays performed in the Middle Ages which taught audiences how to behave through repenting the deadly sins. In 'An Inspector Calls', Eric Birling represents the deadly sin of lust and his relationship with Daisy begins with this base desire.

 ## Grade 9 Exploration: Look at the text in a different way

Does 'An Inspector Calls' offer any positive view on relationships?

Yes: There seems to be hope that Gerald and Sheila might be able to resume their relationship, now based on honesty. Gerald does admit his mistake in Act 3, saying **'I did keep a girl last summer. I've admitted it. And I'm sorry, Sheila'**. The simple *declarative sentences* indicate a genuine, heartfelt apology and an openness and honesty that was missing at the start of the play.

No: Gerald's last words of the play **'What about this ring?'** show his arrogance as he expects everything to return to normal and for Sheila to continue with their marriage plans. His question sounds off-hand and complacent. He has shrugged off the horror of the evening's revelations and is keen to resume his old life, unaffected by the events. Overall, the play shows us relationships which fall apart as the characters' hypocrisies and lies are exposed; relationships based on inequality, lust and desire for status.

> Gerald belonged to the aristocratic class which had a vested interest in maintaining the status quo. The First World War shattered this status quo, with 17% of the aristocratic officers being killed on the battlefields. Priestley wrote the play in 1945, the last year of the Second World War; he was keen to ensure that society started afresh and did not revert to the old ways. Gerald's narrow-minded, complacent attitude jars with the audience in his desire for Sheila to take back the ring.

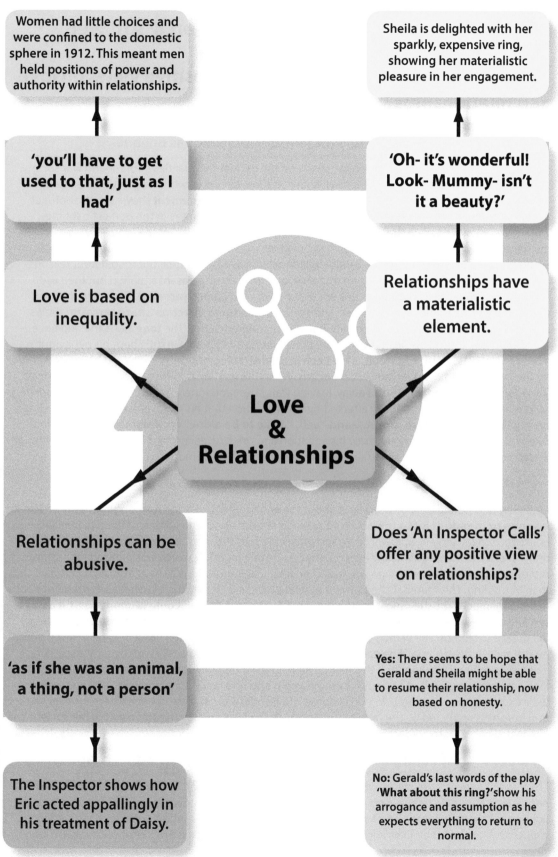

Women had little choices and were confined to the domestic sphere in 1912. This meant men held positions of power and authority within relationships.

Sheila is delighted with her sparkly, expensive ring, showing her materialistic pleasure in her engagement.

'you'll have to get used to that, just as I had'

'Oh- it's wonderful! Look- Mummy- isn't it a beauty?'

Love is based on inequality.

Relationships have a materialistic element.

Love & Relationships

Relationships can be abusive.

Does 'An Inspector Calls' offer any positive view on relationships?

'as if she was an animal, a thing, not a person'

Yes: There seems to be hope that Gerald and Sheila might be able to resume their relationship, now based on honesty.

The Inspector shows how Eric acted appallingly in his treatment of Daisy.

No: Gerald's last words of the play **'What about this ring?'** show his arrogance and assumption as he expects everything to return to normal.

Sample GCSE Exam Question & Answer

Q: Does 'An Inspector Calls' offer any positive views on love and relationships?

☑ Make the point that Priestley presents relationships as unequal

The relationships in the play are unequal, based on the gender inequalities of pre-world war society. Mrs Birling tells her daughter that Sheila will have to allow Gerald to work long hours away from her: **'you'll have to get used to that, just as I had'**. The *declarative statement* shows a matter-of-fact *tone* of acceptance which illustrates how women were expected to stay in the domestic sphere while it was men who were the powerful, dynamic people of business. Yet the long absences in the marriage may well have damaged the Birlings' marriage. Certainly their marriage does not seem one based on much warmth. Daisy and Gerald's relationship was also unequal but for different reasons. Gerald was in a position of power as he rescued Daisy from an unpleasant situation but then used her as his mistress. Sheila highlights this when she says, with **(sharp sarcasm) 'You were the wonderful Fairy Prince'**. She is bitter in her statement and the *stage direction* 'sharp sarcasm' shows how disillusioned Sheila has become with her well-mannered fiance. The *tone* alerts the audience that Gerald has abused his position and that there was nothing **'wonderful'** about his behaviour. As a poor girl in 1912, Daisy/Eva would have been in a vulnerable position and it would have been easy for the wealthy Gerald to take advantage of this. When the relationship runs its course, Gerald gives Daisy some money and then walks away, leaving Daisy hurt and lonely. Yet, Gerald is not a completely callous monster; he is emotionally affected by the realisation that his ex-lover has committed suicide, saying, **'As I'm rather more- upset...-and- well, I'd like to be alone'**. The *fragmented speech* indicated by the *ellipsis* and *dashes* show his agitation and grief, revealing that their relationship, though flawed and ultimately doomed to fail, was one based on genuine emotion.

☑ Make the point that relationships are based on material considerations

Mr Birling tells Gerald how pleased he is about the engagement, saying **'Your engagement to Sheila means a tremendous lot to me'** and continues his speech about the joining of the two families, finishing with talking about lower costs and prices. He sees the relationship, in part, as a business transaction. The marriage will ally the two families closely together which will be good for business. It is probable that his own marriage was based on financial transactions as he is from a lower social class than Mrs Birling. This materialistic element to relationships is also evident in Sheila's excitement about her engagement ring, showing it to her mother: **'Oh- it's wonderful! Look- Mummy- isn't it a beauty?'** She is clearly delighted with it, her *fragmented speech* indicated through the *dashes* showing her great excitement. She warms to Gerald, forgetting about the tension caused by his evasion about his distance in the summer. She comes across as shallow as she is so easily won over by a sparkling expensive ring and we wonder if this relationship is based on material considerations rather than true love. Yet there were limited options for employment and education for women in 1912 and women were expected to marry and bring up children. Sheila might be shallow in her excitement over the ring but she is restricted by the time period in which she lives and, by the standards of her society, she has achieved highly by securing a wealthy husband.

☑ Move to the point that the Inspector exposes the cracks within relationships

The Inspector reveals the cracks within existing relationships and forces the characters to acknowledge truths about old relationships. The *stage directions* indicate how, when he comes on stage, the lighting becomes **'brighter and harder'**, showing how he turns a spotlight on the characters and exposes the truth of their lives and relationships. An example of this is Eric's relationship with Daisy;

he does admit that he forced himself into Eva/Daisy's house and also forced her to have sex, as he was drunk and on the verge of violence **'in that state when a chap easily turns nasty'**. The relationship with Daisy was one based on sex, violence and abuse of power. Yet he uses the *noun* **'chap'** to describe himself; it has the effect of making him sound jolly and rather harmless. Later, the Inspector tells him categorically that his behaviour was disgusting, that Eric treated Daisy **'as if she was an animal, a thing, not a person'**. The *list* shows how Eric abused his position as a rich man of great privilege by diminishing a lonely, poor girl and seeing her as sub-human- an **'animal'** and even an object - **'a thing'**. The Inspector's clear, damning *vocabulary* is a long way from Eric's **'chap'**. Priestley drew upon conventions of morality plays; these were plays performed in the Middle Ages which taught audiences how to behave through repenting the deadly sins. In 'An Inspector Calls', Eric Birling represents the deadly sin of lust and his relationship with Daisy begins with this base desire.

☑ Explore whether there is any hope for relationships at the end of the play

At the end of the play, there seems to be hope that Gerald and Sheila might be able to resume their relationship, now based on honesty. Gerald does admit his mistake in Act 3, saying **'I did keep a girl last summer. I've admitted it. And I'm sorry, Sheila'**. The simple *declarative sentences* indicate a genuine, heartfelt apology and an openness and honesty that was missing at the start of the play. Yet this is only one view and Gerald's last words of the play - **'What about this ring?'** - show his arrogance as he expects everything to return to normal and for Sheila to continue with their marriage plans. His question sounds off-hand and complacent; he has shrugged off the horror of the evening's revelations and is keen to resume his old life, unaffected by the events. Gerald belonged to the aristocratic class which had a vested interest in maintaining the status quo. The First World War shattered this status quo, with 17% of the aristocratic officers being killed on the battlefields. Priestley wrote the play in 1945, the last year of the Second World War; he was keen to ensure that society started afresh and did not revert to the old ways. Gerald's narrow-minded, complacent attitude jars with the audience in his desire for Sheila to take back the ring. Overall, Priestley seems to show a rather bleak view of human love as the play shows us relationships which fall apart as the characters' hypocrisies and lies are exposed: relationships that are based on inequality, lust and desire for status.

Essential Exam Tips

☑ **Check with your exam board or your teacher about what is being assessed in your 'An Inspector Calls' response. For example, depending on your exam board, you might not have to write about context.**

☑ **Some exam boards will ask you to respond to an extract as well as write about the whole text. If you have an extract question, try to make at least four separate points based on the extract.**

Act One

'brighter and harder'
The opening stage directions tell us that the lighting should become **'brighter and harder'** when the Inspecor enters.

'good solid furniture' 'champagne glasses'
The opening stage directions establish the wealth of the Birling family.

'easy well-bred young man-about-town'
The opening stage direction establishes Gerald as a confident, privileged man.

'you'll have to get used to that, just as I had'
Sybil warns her daughter that Sheila will have to get used to Gerald working long hours.

'when you never came near me, and I wondered what had happened to you'
Sheila refers to the summer when Gerald had been inexplicably distant.

'You're squiffy'
Sheila states very clearly that Eric is 'squiffy' after Eric laughs and then quickly suppresses this laugh.

'Your engagement to Sheila means a tremendous lot to me'
Mr Birling tells Gerald how pleased he is about the engagement,

'Oh- it's wonderful! Look- Mummy- isn't it a beauty?'
Sheila is excited about her engagement ring, showing it to her mother.

'I'm talking as a hard-headed, practical man of business'
Arthur Birling declares himself to be a sensible, pragmatic businessman.

'Unsinkable- absolutely unsinkable'
Mr Birling declares the Titanic to be unsinkable.

'So long as we behave ourselves, don't get into the police court or start a scandal- eh? (laughs complacently)
Arthur Birling predicts that his knighthood is almost guaranteed.

'community and all that nonsense'
Mr Birling states that we only have a responsibility to ourselves and to our families.

'sharp ring of a front door bell'
A stage direction of a ringing door bell introduces the Inspector.

'He says his name's Inspector Goole'
The servant Edna announces the Inspector, who claims that his name is 'Goole'.

'impression of massiveness' 'takes charge' 'cutting in'
Stage directions show that the Inspector is in control.

'Burnt her inside out, of course'
Inspector Goole establishes the victim's death: Eva swallowed disinfectant.

'one line of enquiry at a time'
The Inspector takes charge of the enquiry.

'Well, it's my duty to keep labour costs down'
Arthur Birling answers the Inspector's question about why he refused Eva's request for a wage increase.

'She'd had a lot to say- far too much'
Mr Birling describes Eva as the articulate ringleader of a group of workers who asked for a wage increase.

'Why shouldn't they try for higher wages? We try for the highest possible prices.'
Eric approves of Eva's attempt to secure a pay rise, saying that Eva was justified in asking for better wages.

'no work, no money coming in, and living in lodgings, with no relatives to help her'
The Inspector describes how Eva was alone and poor.

'I haven't done anything. She is upsetting herself'
The Inspector says that Sheila is crying because of her own guilt.

'I felt rotten about it at the time'
Sheila admits to feeling guilty about her treatment of Eva Smith.

Act Two

'Girls of that class'
Mrs Birling dismisses Eva Smith as **'girls of that class'**.

'Young and fresh and charming'
Gerald describes Daisy as **'young and fresh and charming'**.

(sharp sarcasm) 'You were the wonderful Fairy Prince'
Sheila is bitter in her statement that Gerald was Daisy's fairy-tale prince.

'As I'm rather more- upset …-and- well, I'd like to be alone'
Gerald is emotionally affected by the realisation that his ex-lover has committed suicide.

'To be alone, to be quiet, to remember'
After Gerald ended their relationship, Eva went away to be by herself.

'twenty-four…very pretty'
Eva is described as young and attractive.

(with dignity)'We've done a great deal of useful work in helping deserving cases'
Mrs Birling is complacent and self-satisfied in her role as head of a charitable organisation.

'Don't stammer and yammer at me, man. I'm losing all patience with you people.'
The Inspector becomes impatient with Mr Birling's interruptions and tells him to be quiet.

'As if a girl of that sort would ever refuse money!'
Mrs Birling laughs at the idea of Daisy turning down the stolen money from Eric.

(With sudden alarm) 'Mother- stop - stop!'
As Mrs Birling begins to unknowingly condemn her own son at the end of Act 2, Sheila tries to stop her.

'compelled to confess in public his responsibility'
Mrs Birling states that the man responsible
for Eva/Daisy's pregnancy should be forced
to publicly admit his guilt.

(agitated) I don't believe it. I **won't** believe
it'
Sybil Birling refuses to believe that her son
is involved with Eva/Daisy and the pregnancy.

Act Three

'Beside, you're not the type- you don't get
drunk-'
Sybil Birling is still in denial about her son's
behaviour.

'I was in that state when a chap easily
turns nasty'
Eric admits that he forced himself into
Daisy's house and also forced her to have
sex, as he was drunk and on the verge of
violence

'I've got to cover this up as soon as I can.
You damned fool-'
Mr Birling's first instinct when he hears
about Eric's activities of stealing money is
to 'cover this up'.

'used her...as if she was an animal, a thing,
not a person'
The Inspector tells Eric clearly how he
abused Daisy.

(unhappily) 'I'd give thousands- yes thousands'
Mr Birling wishes that he could change the
events.

'millions and millions and millions of Eva
Smiths'
The Inspector tells us that there are many
more women like Eva Smith needing help.

'We don't live alone. We are members
of one body. We are responsible for one
another'
The Inspector gives clear messages about
responsibility.

'Fire and blood and anguish'
The Inspector's final speech warns that, if
society does not learn lessons of public and
private responsibility for the poor and the
weak, then it will be taught these lessons in
'fire and blood and anguish'.

(bitterly) I suppose we're all nice people
now'
Sheila's ironic tone shows just how much
she has changed from the beginning of the
play as she is fully aware that the actions of
herself and her family were unjustifiable.

'I did keep a girl last summer. I've admitted it. And I'm sorry, Sheila'.
Gerald admits his mistake.

(shouting) And I say the girl's dead and
we all helped to kill her- and that's what
matters-'
By the end of Act 3, Eric has changed from
the unconfident boy we see in Act 1; here
he admits that he killed Eva, blames his
family as well and dismisses his father's
concerns over public exposure.

'They just won't try to... see the difference between a lot of stuff like this coming out in private and a downright public scandal'
At the end, when it is realised that the Inspector was a 'fake', Birling sneers at his children for still being troubled by the evening's events.

'Fire and blood and anguish. And it frightens me the way you talk'
At the end of Act 3, Sheila remembers the Inspector's warning and is worried at how her parents have been unaffected by the evening's events.

'What about this ring?'
Gerald's last words of the play show his arrogance as he expects everything to return to normal and for Sheila to resume their relationship.

Glossary
Explanation of terms

Adjective - a word that describes a noun **e.g. 'I'm talking as a <u>hard-headed, practical </u>man of business.'**

Adverb - a word that gives information about a verb **e.g. 'sulkily'**

Anaphora - repetition of the first part of a sentence **e.g. 'no work, no money coming in'**

Auxiliary verb - a verb used to clarify the main verb **e.g. 'I don't believe it'**

Climax - the most exciting part of a story or play

Colloquial phrase - everyday language **e.g. 'Don't... yammer at me, man'**

Contrast/juxtaposition - use of opposites **e.g. the 'good solid furniture' of the Birlings contrasts with Eva's 'lodgings'.**

Dash - punctuation mark that breaks up a sentence or phrase **e.g.' I'd give thousands- yes, thousands'**

Declarative sentence - a sentence that declares an idea or opinion **e.g. 'We all helped kill her.'**

Determiner - word that defines a noun **e.g. 'I did keep <u>a</u> girl last summer'**

Dramatic irony - when the audience knows something the characters do not **e.g. only the audience understands how foolish Arthur Birling sounds when he declares the Titanic to be unsinkable.**

Ellipsis - a punctuation mark which suggests a sentence is unfinished

Everyman - the character in a morality play who represents the common man/woman

Exposition - the beginning of a play or story

Falling action - the part of the play or story after the climax

Foreshadowing - to give a warning of a future event **e.g. 'sharp ring' of the doorbell foreshadows how the Inspector will disturb the Birlings.**

Fragmented speech - speaking in short, incomplete sentences **e.g.' I'd give thousands- yes, thousands'**

Juxtaposition - see contrast

Imperative verbs - verbs that give orders **e.g. '<u>Don't</u> stammer and yammer at me, man'**

Inclusive pronoun - use of first person plural pronouns to create a sense of community **e.g. 'We are all members of one body'**

Interjection - an added word or phrase to a sentence **e.g. 'Burnt her inside out, of course.'**

Intensifier - a word that gives emphasis **e.g. 'unsinkable, absolutely unsinkable'**

Noun - name of an object/place/time/emotion **e.g. 'fire'**

Pace - the speed or rate at which the story unfolds

Plot device - technique used to move narrative along

Repetition - when a word or phrase is repeated **e.g. 'unsinkable, absolutely unsinkable'**

Rising action - part of a story or play which has events building up

Resolution - the conclusion of a play when conflict is resolved

Setting - where a scene is played out e.g. the setting of the play is in the Birlings' house.

Stage direction - instruction in the play to the actors or director

Structure - the order in which a line/scene/play is put together

Symbol - when an object/person stands for something else **e.g. Sheila is a symbol of hope.**

Syndetic list - a list where the items are separated with a conjunction **e.g. 'fire and blood and anguish'.**

Tone - mood or atmosphere or voice

Verb - an action word **e.g. Mrs Birling says that the father of Daisy's baby should be 'compelled' to confess in public**

Vocabulary - word choices

Lightning Source UK Ltd.
Milton Keynes UK
UKHW050003060320
359862UK00003B/20